AN ESSENTIAL IN PUBLIC HEALTH AND EPIDEMIOLOGY

MIHIR BHATTA

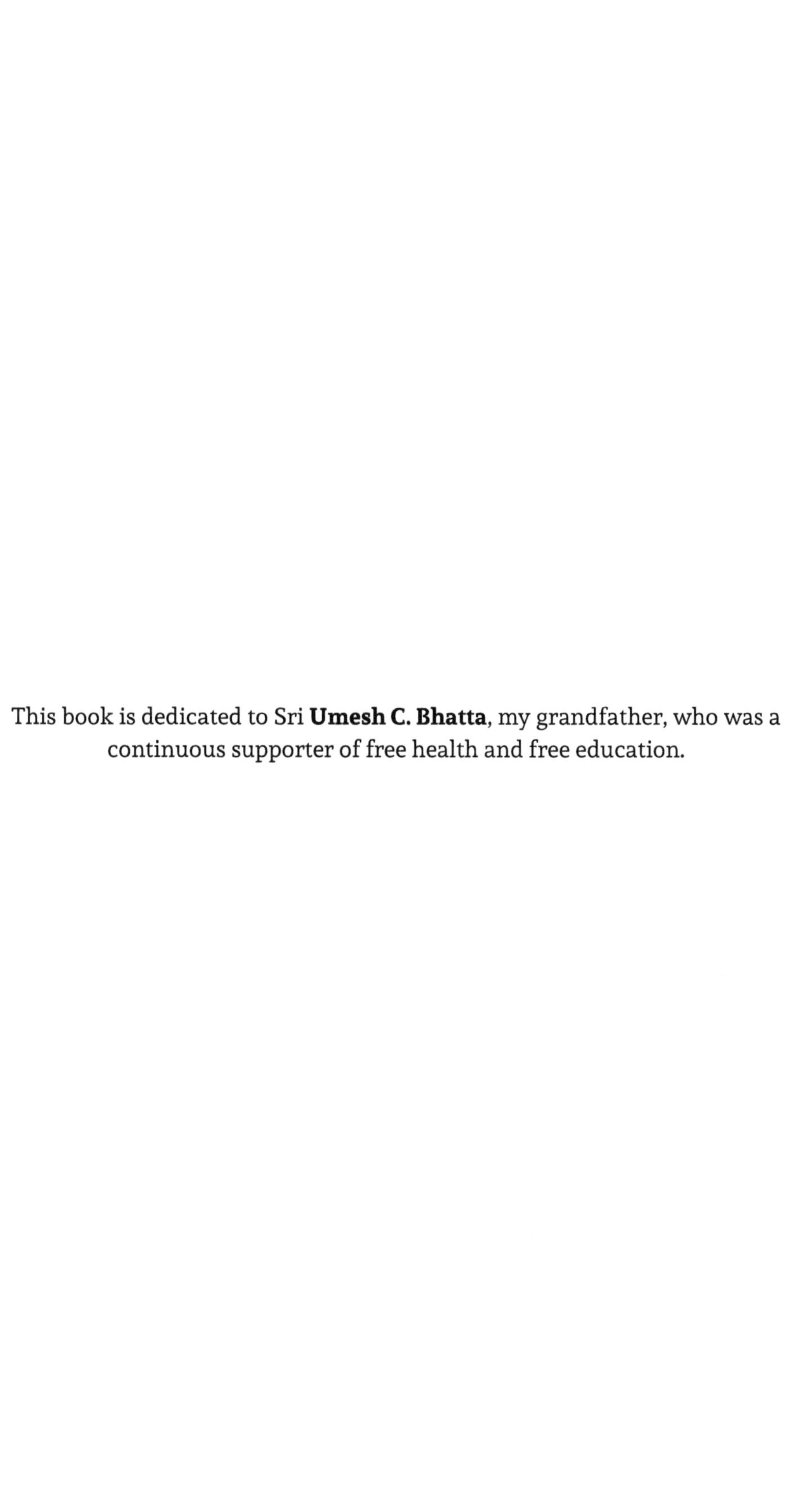

This book is dedicated to Sri **Umesh C. Bhatta**, my grandfather, who was a continuous supporter of free health and free education.

Contents

"You don't have to burn books to destroy a culture. Just get people to stop reading them."

Ray Bradbury

FOREWORD

Mihir was one of my students during his Master's. He is a trained fellow in Molecular Biology and Genetics during his days in Presidency College. After that, he opted for Ph.D. But for his thesis, he had to work in the field of Geographical Information System (GIS) for Livestock Developments. He also works in the field of determination of drainage or basin through satellite imagery of IRS LISS IV data, artificial and natural recharge systems, etc. In the later period of work, he was moved to computational biology. After completing his Doctoral degree, he join medical research and published several articles in Systematic Reviews along with Meta-analysis. Moreover, he had written a book on this subject also.

The present book on Public Health and Epidemiology is also a good depiction of him. Here he is trying to accumulate all the information regarding Public Health and Epidemiology. At present, there are several books available on Public Health, Epidemiology, or Community Health in e-markets. Those books are for the people who are in the field of Public Health, Epidemiology, or Community Health for quite some time. This book will be helpful to the budding epidemiologist, who has no academic training on this subject. This book will also be helpful to the teachers for subject development, and exam purposes.

I wish him a grand success, like all his previously published books.

-

-

Prof. (Dr.) TK Mukherjee
Retd. Professor, Dept. of Entomology
Presidency College, Kolkata

ACKNOWLEDGEMENTS

I like to thank Dr. TK Mukherjee, for not only forwarding my book but through his competent eyes we visualized the subject of vector biology and community health. He is one of the best Professors in Entomology/ Medical Entomology during his tenure. I would like to thank the Director, ICMR-NICED along with Dr. Agniva Majumdar, Scientist, ICMR-NICED, and Director General, NACO, Government of India.

I would like to mention the name Dr. Alok Deb, Dr. Subrata Biswas, Dr. M.K. Saha, Dr. Debjit Chakraborty, Dr. Falguni Debnath, Dr. Santanu Banerjee, Dr. Sitikhanta Banerjee, Dr. Debdutta Agasty, DR. Rohini Chakraborty, Mr. Anshuman Mandal, Mr. Pankaj Khan, Mr. Rajesh Das, and Miss. Piyali the division of virology and division of epidemiology of ICMR-NICED, Kolkata for their continuous encouragement and support. I like to thank my teacher Prof. (Dr.) Kedarnath Bhattacharjee, Dr. Kautilya Bhattacherjee, Mr. Amit Sircar, Prof. D. Das, and Prof. PR Ghosh.

Here I like to mention the name of Subham, Mr. Mrityunjay, and Mrs. Saswati for their continuous encouragement. I would like to mention my family, my sister Mou, mother Purnima, my father Manik C. Bhatta, and my wife Manisha, who always stands beside me in every harsh situation. Also, like to thank each and every budding researcher in this relevant field. I will be glad if anybody learns anything from this book.

-

-

Mihir Bhatta

Ph.D., PGDPHM, DSSi, FCRSD, FSASS

PREFACE

At present, there are many good epidemiology textbooks on the market, but most of these are addressed to students of public health or people who do clinical research with epidemiologic methods. There is a need for a short introduction on how epidemiologic methods are used in public health, and genetic and clinical epidemiology because health professionals need to know basic epidemiologic methods covering etiologic as well as prognostic factors of diseases. They need to know more about methodology than introductory texts on public health have to offer. In some health faculties, epidemiology is not even part of the teaching curriculum.

We believe this to be a serious mistake. Medical students are students of all aspects of diseases and health. Without knowing something about epidemiology the clinicians and other health professionals cannot read a growing part of the scientific literature in any reasonably critical way and cannot navigate the world of "evidence-based medicine and evidence-based prevention." Without skills in epidemiologic methodology, they are in the hands of experts that may not only have an interest in health. Some health professionals may believe that only common sense is needed to conduct epidemiological studies, but the scientific literature and the public debate on health issues indicate that common sense is often in short supply and may not thrive without some formal training. Epidemiologic methods play a key role in identifying environmental, social, and genetic determinants of diseases. Clinical epidemiology addresses the transition from disease to health or toward mortality or social or medical handicaps.

Public health epidemiology addresses the transition from being healthy to being not healthy. Descriptive epidemiology provides the disease pattern that is needed to look at health from a broad perspective and to set the priorities right. Epidemiology is a basic science of medicine that addresses key questions such as "Who becomes ill?" and "What are important prognostic factors?" Answers to such questions provide the basis for better prevention and treatment of diseases.

During my course on PGDPHM (Postgraduate Diploma in Public Health Management), I needed a compact book, from which a person like me who belongs to nonepidemiological background can start. These incidents compelled me to address the situation. As only weapon I have to fight is the pen (now keyboard). The present book is written, sharing my understanding of the subject, current up-to-date information, and present-day research on Clinical Epidemiology in Public Health concern.

.

.

Mihir Bhatta

June, 2022
Kolkata

PROLOGUE

A blue plaque was installed by the Royal Society of Chemistry to honour Dr. John Snow for his work during the Broad Street outbreak, 1854

Dr. John Snow (15 March 1813 – 16 June 1858) was an English physician and a leader in the development of anesthesia and medical hygiene. He is considered one of the founders of modern epidemiology, in part because of his work in tracing the source of a cholera outbreak in Soho, London, in 1854, which he curtailed by removing the handle of a water pump. Snow's findings inspired the adoption of anaesthesia as well as fundamental changes in the water and waste systems of London, which led to similar changes in other cities, and a significant improvement in general public health around the world.

An Essential in Public Health and Epidemiology

I

Introduction

Definition

Public health has been defined as "the science and art of preventing disease", prolonging life and improving quality of life through organized efforts and informed choices of society, organizations (public and private), communities and individuals. The public can be as small as a handful of people or as large as a village or an entire city. The concept of health takes into account physical, psychological, and social well-being. As such, according to the World Health Organization, "health is a state of complete physical, mental and social well-being and not merely the absence of disease or infirmity".

Public health has been defined as "the science and art of preventing disease, prolonging life and promoting health through the organized efforts and informed choices of society, organizations, public and private, communities and individuals". Analyzing the determinants of health of a population and the threats it faces is the basis for public health. The public can be as small as a handful of people or as large as a village or an entire city; in the case of a pandemic, it may encompass several continents. The concept of health takes into account physical, psychological, and social well-being.

Public health is an interdisciplinary field. For example, epidemiology, biostatistics, social sciences and management of health services are all relevant. Other important sub-fields include environmental health, community health, behavioral health, health economics, public policy, mental health, health education, health politics, occupational safety, disability, oral health, gender issues in health, and sexual and reproductive health. Public health, together with primary care, secondary care, and tertiary care, is part of a country's overall health care system. Public health is implemented through the surveillance of cases and health indicators, and through the promotion of healthy behaviors. Common public health initiatives include promotion of hand-washing and breastfeeding, delivery of vaccinations, promoting ventilation and improved air quality both indoors and outdoors, suicide prevention, smoking cessation, obesity education, increasing healthcare accessibility and distribution of condoms to control the spread of sexually transmitted diseases.

There is a significant disparity in access to health care and public health initiatives between developed countries and developing countries, as well as within developing countries. In developing countries, public health infrastructures are still forming. There may not be enough trained healthcare workers, monetary resources, or, in some cases, sufficient knowledge to provide even a basic level of medical care and disease prevention. Major public health concern in developing countries is poor maternal and child health, exacerbated by malnutrition and poverty coupled with governments' reluctance in implementing public health policies.

From the beginnings of human civilization, communities promoted health and fought disease at the population level. In complex, pre-industrialized societies, interventions designed to reduce health risks could be the initiative of different stakeholders, such as army generals, the clergy or rulers. Great Britain became a leader in the development of public health initiatives, beginning in the 19th century, due to the fact that it was the first modern urban nation worldwide. The public health initiatives that began to emerge initially focused on sanitation (for example, the Liverpool and London sewerage systems), control of infectious diseases (including vaccination and quarantine) and an evolving infrastructure of various sciences, e.g. statistics, microbiology, epidemiology, sciences of engineering.

Defining what public health is?

Many of us can consider that some of these definitions contain the term 'medicine' whereas others don't. This is a reflection of two contradictory directions that have been pulled on public health as a discipline for centuries. One concept of public health is based on a broad focus on the underlying social and economic causes of health and disease and their variation in populations. The other has a narrower medical focus with the treatment of ill health at its centre. You have noticed the terms like 'state medicine' or 'complete medical police' which sound a bit awkward in this day and age. The organization of public health structures has always been closely related to the way communities and societies organize themselves, which role was allocated to the ruling class in looking after the well-being of citizens, and which responsibilities were allocated to citizens themselves. In the following we provide you with two modern definitions of what public health is about. The first is from the 1987 UK Acheson Report which looked into the future of the public health function: 'Public Health is the art and science of preventing disease, promoting health and prolonging life through organised efforts of society'. Beaglehole and Bonita's book Public Health at the Crossroads, published in 2004, defines public health as 'Collective action for sustained population-wide health improvement'.

Characteristics and components

Public health is a complex term, composed of many elements and different practices. It is a multi-faceted, interdisciplinary field. For example, epidemiology, biostatistics, social sciences and management of health services are all relevant. Other important sub-fields include environmental health, community health, behavioral health, health economics, public policy, mental health, health education, health politics, occupational safety, disability, gender issues in health, and sexual and reproductive health.

Modern public health practice requires multidisciplinary teams of public health workers and professionals. Teams might include epidemiologists, biostatisticians, physician assistants, public health nurses, midwives, medical microbiologists, pharmacists, economists, sociologists, geneticists, data managers, environmental health officers (public health inspectors), bioethicists, gender experts, sexual and reproductive health specialists, physicians, and veterinarians. The elements and priorities of public health have evolved over time, and are continuing to evolve. Different regions in the world can have different public health concerns at a given time. Common public health initiatives include promotion of hand-washing and breastfeeding, delivery of vaccinations, suicide prevention, smoking cessation, obesity education, increasing healthcare accessibility and distribution of condoms to control the spread of sexually transmitted diseases.

History of public health

If diseases are known to be preventable, society may decide to give a role to certain public health professionals to make sure that people remain healthy for longer. This may either be prompted by concern for their health per se or by a desire to reduce poverty by keeping people healthy enough to work, or it could be prompted by a desire to keep civil order. Chinese medicine, Ayurvedic medicine in India (400 BC), Hippocrates in Greece (460–377 BC) and Galen (AD 129–199) in Rome and their followers were aware of the influences of season, diet, the winds and lifestyle for individual people's health. Galen created the theory of 'miasma' or bad air causing disease. A miasma was seen as consisting of malodorous and poisonous particles created by decomposing organic matter. For hundreds of years, the 'miasma' theory competed with the theory of contagion. This contagion theory had its origin in the success of the ancient practice of isolating ill people. The discovery of the microscope in 1683 was followed by the discovery of micro-organisms in the late nineteenth century. These discoveries drastically changed the theory of disease causation and the 'contagion theory' dominated public health thinking between the late nineteenth century and the mid-twentieth century. Theories of disease causation, the disease is seen as preventable, together with a high level of organization of society, were required in designing systematic approaches to disease prevention. They were targeted at fighting major disease outbreaks such as plagues and leprosy. Between 1347 and 1351 the plague or the 'Black Death' killed approximately one-third (23 million) of the total population of Europe's 80 million people within only a three-year period. While medical Islamic doctors had developed the science of hygiene to a very high level, they agreed with their Christian counterparts that plagues were God-given and should not be fought.

During sixteenth century

In the then city states Milan and Florence of Italy, during sixteenth century that the concepts of purification of enclosed space – quarantine, a 40-day hold on ships, and isolation of victims, washing surfaces with lime and vinegar – were developed for the protection of wealthy citizens. These cities also began providing 'lazarettes' to house plague victims and for the first time created semi-permanent public health posts to enforce plague regulations. The concept of the dirtiness of air as being the root cause of disease outbreaks is reflected in two seventeenth-century documents from Britain: John Evelyn's '*Fumifugium or the Inconvenience of the Air and Smoke of London Dissipated*' and John Graunt's '*The Nature and Political Observations made upon the Bills of Mortality*' (1662). After the forests around London had been cut down, the resulting energy crisis was met by importing sea-coal from Newcatle in the north-east of England. Newcastle upon Tyne, the city of origin of sea-coal, is the city where this study guide is being written. This is one of the early accounts linking air pollution with the health of populations, in this case the residents of London and Newcastle.

During twentieth century

While early epidemiology was dominated by infectious diseases, the early twentieth century saw some consideration of non-infectious causes of disease. The American Joseph Goldberger concluded in 1914 and then in 1930 that pellagra was not an infectious disease but was due to diet (later determined as lack of vitamin B). In the past 50 years many investigations linking non-communicable diseases with health outcomes have centred around personal behaviours, often couched as behaviour choices. Such behaviours in turn have been the focus of much public health practice (smoking, alcohol intake, obesity, levels of physical activity). Epidemiological studies have made great contributions towards unravelling the complex interplay of a range of risk factors. However, they have often failed to consider broader environmental and social determinants of health behaviour. Many prevention programmes have taken the form of blaming and stigmatizing individuals for their unhealthy habits without considering wider social factors that underpin lifestyle choices.

Recent developments

Over the past 20 years or so a range of molecular techniques have been added to the portfolio that epidemiologists use to link exposure with disease information. Measuring a potentially harmfully substance in blood, urine, or teeth allows one to consider jointly all routes of exposure, be it inhalation, uptake via food and water (oral), or via the skin (dermal). Measuring the early response within a critical target organ is conceptually a very attractive way of improving the quality of exposure assessment. However, in practice, the applications of biomarkers of exposure have been much more limited for a number of reasons. These include their often short biological half-life which means that only exposure in the recent past can be investigated. Often it is not yet well understood what the markers are actually measuring. The role of individual susceptibility to cancer-causing agents and the development of molecular techniques to identify individual strains of bacteria through their genome sequence promised a big surge in the proportion of explained disease variation some years back. However, even for such an intensely studied disease as breast cancer the currently six identified genes explain only approximately 20 percent of the aggregation of breast cancer in families. In the developed world it is likely that molecular and genetic epidemiology and biological monitoring research will continue for quite a while. In terms of methods for improving global public health, it is much more likely, that broad public health evidence-based measures such as the millennium development goals on child mortality, maternal health, environmental sustainability, poverty and gender equality will impact much more on the global burden of disease. In parallel to the changing paradigms and theories that have underpinned public health practice and epidemiology, there have also been changes in the nature of the evidence that impacts public health practices.

Major Disciplinies

1. Nutrition: is the science of food, the nutrients and other substances therein, and their action, interaction and balance in relation to health and disease.
2. Reproductive health: is a state of complete physical, mental and social being not only absence of disease or infirmity, but in all matters relating to the reproductive system and to its functions and process.
3. Environmental Health: The basic approach to environmental control is first to identify specific biological, chemical, social and physical factors that represent hazards to health or well-being and to modify the environment in a manner that protects people from harmful exposures. The principal components of environmental health are water sanitation,

waste disposal , etc.

4. Health Education: is defined as a combination of learning experiences designed to facilitate voluntary actions conducive to health. It is an essential part of health promotion.
5. Epidemiology: are the study of frequency, distribution, and determinants of diseases and other related states or events in specified populations. The application of this study to the promotion of health and to the prevention and control of health problems is evident.
6. Health Economics: is concerned with the alternative uses of resources in the health services sector and with the efficient utilization of economic resources such as manpower, material and financial resources.
7. Biostatistics: is the application of statistics to biological problems; application of statistics especially to medical problems, but its real meaning is broader.
8. Health Service Management: is getting people to work harmoniously together and to make efficient use of resources in order to achieve objectives.
9. Ecology: is the study of relationships between living organisms and their environment. It is the science, that deals with the inter-relationships between the various organisms living in an area and their relationship with the physical environment. Human ecology means the study of human groups as influenced by environmental factors, including social and behavioral factors.
10. Demography: is the study of population, especially with reference to size and density, fertility, mortality, growth, age distribution, migration, and the interaction of all those with social and economic conditions

II

Cultural Influence: Health Care Practice

Definition

Culture is that complex whole that includes knowledge, belief, art, morals, law, customs and other capabilities and habits acquired by man as a member of society. Culture refers to the sum total of the life- ways of a group of people who share values, beliefs and practices that are passed on form generation to generation and which change through time.

Culture is the sum total of the things that people do because of having been taught. For the perpetuation of the human race, man depends on culture, which is a learned behavior. Culture is peculiar to human beings. It separates man and society from that of animals and insects, whose behavior is always only instinctual and therefore does not change. Man's culture or learned behavior makes it possible to change continuously.

The suggested levels of culture

Concrete

The most visible tangible artifacts such as clothes, music, art, food and games. Festivals and celebrations focus on these dimensions.

Behavioral

Behavioral practices reflect values and defined social and gender roles, languages spoken, and approaches to non-verbal communication. Behavioral aspects of culture include language, gender roles, family structure, political affiliation, and community organization.

Symbolic

Symbolic values and beliefs are often expressed in symbols and rituals. Although often abstract, symbolic meaning is key to how people define themselves in relation to each other, the world and the universe. Symbolic expression includes value systems, religion, worldview, customs, spirituality, morals and ethics.

Relation of Culture and Health

Culture is one of the determinants of health among the environmental factors. An individual's culture influences his or her attitude toward various health issues, including perceptions of what is and is not a health problem, methods of disease prevention, treatment of illness, and use of health providers. In every culture, the care of the sick person is clearly dictated not only as to what care he/she is given, but also who will do it and how he/she should proceed. We learn from our own cultural and ethnic backgrounds how to be healthy, how to recognize illness, and how to be ill. Meanings attached to the notions of health and illnesses are related to basic, culture-bound values by which we define a given experience and perceptions.

People around the world have beliefs and behaviors related to health and illness that stem from cultural forces and individual experience and perceptions. To understand the cultural context of health, it is essential to work with several key concepts:

Insider and outsider concept

Perspectives are useful for examining when we are seeing things from our point of view and when we are trying to understand someones else's view of things. Insider shows the culture as viewed from within. It refers to the meaning that people attach to things from their cultural perspective. For example, the view of worms (*Ascaris*) in children are normal and are caused by eating sweets in the perspective within some cultures. The outsider perspective refers to something as seen from the outside. Rather than meaning, it conveys a structural approach or something as seen without understanding its meaning for a culture. It can also convey an outsider's meaning attached to the same phenomenon. For example, *Ascaris* is contracted through eggs ingested by contact with contaminated soil or foods contaminated by contact with that soil. . The concept of insider and outsider perspective allows us to look at health, illness and prevention and treatment systems from several perspectives; to analyze the differences between these perspectives; and to develop approaches that will work within a cultural context. The insider-outsider concept leads to other sets of concepts. Disease in the insider, usually the western biomedical definition refers to an undesirable deviation from a measurable norm. Example deviation in temperature, white cell counts and many others are seen as indicators of disease. Illness, on the other hand, means "not feeling well." thus, it is a subjective, insider view. This setups some immediate dissonance between the two views. It is possible to have an undesirable deviation from a western biomedical norm and to feel fine. For example, hypertension, early-stage of cancer. HIV infection and early stages of diabetes are all instances where people might feel well, in spite of having a disease. This means that health care providers "fix" something that people may not realize is wrong. It is also possible for someone to feel ill and for the western biomedical system not to identify a disease.

Ethnocentrisms

Ethnocentrisms refer to seeing one's culture as "best". This is a natural tendency, because the survival and perpetuation of a culture depend on teaching children to accept it and on its members feeling that it is a good thing. Cultural relativism in anthropology refers to the idea that each culture has developed its own ways of solving problems of how to live together; how to obtain the essentials of life, such as food and shelter; how to explain phenomena; and so on. No one is "better" or "worse"; they are just different. This is a challenge, what if a behavior is "wrong" from and epidemiological perspective. How does one distinguish between a 'dangerous' behavior (example, using HIV contaminated needle) and behavior that are merely different and therefore, seems odd? For example, Bolivian peasants use very fine clay in a drink believed to be good for digestion and stomach ailments. Health workers succeeded in discouraging this practice in some communities because 'eating dirt' seemed like a bad thing. The health workers then found themselves faced with increased caries (tooth decay) and other symptoms of calcium deficiency. Upon analysis, the clay was a key source of calcium for these communities. Thus, there is a delicate balance between being judgmental without good reason and introducing behavior change because there is real harm from Introduction to existing behaviors. In general, it is best to live harmless practices alone and focus on understanding and changing harmful behaviors.

Holism concept

The concept of holism is also useful in looking at health and disease cross-culturally. Holism is an approach used by anthropologists that looks at the broad context of whatever phenomenon is being studied. Holism involves staying alert for unexpected influences because one never knows what may have a bearing on the program one is trying to implement. For public health, this is crucial because there may be diverse factors influencing health and health behavior.

III

Health Care: Traditional Practices

Introduction

Nowadays, there is a mix of western biomedicine and indigenous practices in health care in different parts of the world, especially in developing counties. Countries like Brazil and China have well-developed traditional medicine in their health care system. Traditional medicine was recognized by the Ministry of Health of Ethiopia as an important alternative health resource readily available to both rural and urban communities. An office for traditional medicine was established in the Ministry of Health of Ethiopia in 1975 with the task of co-coordinating nationalized activities. This includes the phytochemical screening of enthobontanical pharmacopeia, clinical evaluation of traditional health practices and surgical procedures, and the census of traditional medical practitioners. Despite all aims, little was accomplished and only traditional birth attendants were trained and employed and some medicinal were screened. Nevertheless, ethnomedical beliefs and practices continue to be widely followed throughout urban and rural Ethiopia, reflecting considerable cultural continuity and the persistent poor accessibility and quality of most modern health services.

In Ethiopia where more than half of the population depends on traditional medicine, involving both the traditional healers and the practice in the health care system is a good opportunity.

Traditional medicine: structural variety

Traditional medicine in Ethiopia is characterized by great variation and has been shaped by a host of ecological, social, cultural and historical factors. First, variation in climate, elevation, topography and soil type play a major role in the frequency and distribution of diseases that traditional medicine is called upon to deal. For example, it is people who are living in hot lands/ low lands who are ethnomedically familiar with visceral leishmaniasis and trypanosomiasis unlike the people living in high lands who have their healing practices on common cold and rheumatism. Second, the multiethnic character of the population and the uniqueness of the individual socio-cultural environments within which it developed have influenced the Ethiopian ethnomedical system. Third, historical developments related to prolonged immigration from different areas surrounding the country such as the southern Arabian Peninsula, the influx of Greek culture, and the introduction of Christianity and Islam have influenced the Ethiopian ethnomedical heritage.

Despite the above-mentioned variation, the Ethiopian ethnomedicine can be described as an integrated system of beliefs and practices, characterized by an internally coherent discourse on health and illness. Illness perception may either promote health-enhancing behaviors, or it can lead to health lowering behaviors and practices. The settlement pattern of Ethiopians concentrated in the highlands is due to the traditional fear of malaria in the lowland; which is an example to health enhancing behavior. Whereas the case of the traditional management of diarrhea in children by mothers in which the Ethiopian mothers believe that diarrhea is caused by teething, to which they respond by limiting food and fluid with the intention of decreasing the volume and frequency of diarrhea is a negative practice. These popular beliefs can affect treatment decision-making. Ethno medical definition of Health In the Ethiopian ethnomedical setting, health is defined as a state of equilibrium among the physiological, spiritual, cosmological, ecological, and social forces surrounding the man.

This state of balance is enhanced by factors of a spiritual behavioral and physiological nature. First wellbeing is thought to be secured by a peaceful relationship with the supernatural world (Sky-God, nature and ancestral sprites, magical agents). Additionally, behavioral modernization is considered as an important promise for health looking. Conversely, any excess in drinking eating working and uncontrolled conditions such as anger/grief may be conducive to ill health. Moreover, a proper functioning of the human body is viewed as being dependent on physiological and adequate food intake. For example in Ethiopian context intestinal worms constitutes an integral part of the human body and when they exceed the ideal number, they can cause ill health. This equilibrium can be rectified through the traditional practice of taking powerful vermifuge (e.g. "Kosso") on a regular base. The desirable state of well-being is disrupted by the onset of sickness. A number of factors influence the formulation of disease ethnologies.

Circumstances surrounding the illness episode Individual subjectivity, opinion of elders and significant others and, demographic status (age, sex, religion) Nonetheless, two broad domains of ethnological theories are identifiable in the Ethiopian ethno-medical system. These are naturalistic and Magico-religious.

Naturalistic ethnology

In this ethological theory, aliments are ascribed to causes pertaining to the empirical domain and exclude the intervention of a supernatural agent. Hence sickness may result from External factors – such as a faulty interaction with the environment, e.g. drinking polluted water, eating unaccustomed or bad food, atmospheric charges, inhaling dust etc. Contagion through physical contact with a sick person, e.g. Sexual relationship, inhaling a sick person's breath, drinking from a sick person's cup Interpersonal conflict, e.g. Wounds provoked by fights and wife beating Personal excesses, e.g. prolonged exposure to sun and rain, bathing in cold water, eating the unripe crop, drinking immoderately

Magico- religious domain

In this domain of etiology for a disease, illnesses are attributed to God, nature and demonic spirites (e.g. "Zar") ancestral ghosts, magical forces (evil eye, curse) and breach of social taboos or personal vows. Violation of religious and social norms is thought to bring about divine retribution in the form of epidemics. Moreover, spirits are believed to seize humans, bringing about prolonged illness while the diagnosis of possession by a spirit generally requires the validation of a ritual expert. Ailments such as mental illness and epilepsy are routinely attributed to the action of an evil spirit. The fear of evil eye and sorcery is widespread in Ethiopia. This phenomenon is known as "Buda" in several Ethiopian Semitic and Cushitic languages and in a variety of terms in some other groups. This is usually associated with predominantly despised artisan castes like potters, tanners, and blacksmiths. Furthermore, sorcery in the Ethiopian socio-cultural context consists of deliberate enticement of magical acts aimed at harming someone. Usually, it takes place in a situation of interpersonal conflicts, social deviance and/or desire for revenge. The deleterious health consequences of sorcery are highly feared and counteracted with appropriate rituals.

In addition to ailments recognized by biomedicine, the Ethiopian ethnic medical system comprises a number of folk syndromes ascribed to both empirical and supernatural etiologies. For example, the Sidamo label the term "ranta" an ailment characterized by chest pain and back pains, fatigue and breathing difficulties. Its ethnology is described in empirical terms, and it is thought to be triggered by excess commonplace activities, e.g. Carrying heavy loads. The prescribed treatment includes drinking goat's blood, eating abundant food, horn cupping, thermal baths and rest.

The traditional perinatal care

The majorities of Ethiopian women deliver at home and follow the traditional birth customs. In this context, traditional birth attendants play an important role in prenatal and perinatal care. These traditional birth attendants possess a vast range of cumulative knowledge in the field of midwifery and gynecological therapy. They are called especially in the event of childbirth complications. They facilitate deliveries through massaging and another form of manipulation, often involving purification of the birth carnal with butter. Traditional beliefs and practices concerning pregnancy and childbirth are also widespread. Ethno medical beliefs predominate in the explanation of conception. For example in Sidamo, conception is thought to derive from the mixing of male seminal fluid with female blood, while the function of female reproductive organs appeared to be ignored. Pregnancy is considered a dangerous state as the fetus could easily pray for evil eye and sorcery. These are believed to cause miscarriage, premature delivery and total malformation.

Preparation for childbirth also entails empirical practices, which aim at enhancing the health of both the expectant mother and the fetus. In some parts of the country, Kembata and Hadya, Kosso is taken at various stages of the pregnancy with the main purpose of cleaning the bowel as it would be "shameful for a woman to show intestinal parasite at birth", "making space for the fetus", and "keeping the fetus weight down" as the delivery of a big baby would cause protracted and painful labor. Varieties of practices are enacted after delivery. The umbilical cord is cut with a razor blade after the placenta is expelled for the stated reason that the neonate needs the blood to breath. The placenta is usually buried out side the house and in Ethiopian culture its burial site has deep symbolic and emotional overtones as it signifies one's roots and desirable place of death. Ethno botanical remedies are also used widely both during pre and postnatal period. Among various groups, fruits are given to expectant mothers as a remedy against eclampsia.

In northern Ethiopia, the newly born baby is generally given some butter after birth so as to clear the baby's intestines from black tar and other fluids accumulated during gestation while colostrums is squeezed out and generally avoided as a potential source of abdominal pains, breast feeding carried out universally beginning the 3rd day of life. The birth of a new baby also results in weaning of the older child, for this purpose a bitter juice is placed on the nipples in order to discourage the baby on breast-feeding.

Secular Healing Many ailments are routinely explained with an empirical framework of illness etiology and treated with curative practices, which do not involve Magico-religious rituals. In this domain various levels of specialization exist, ranging from home remedies to professional treatment.

Self-care by households

Self-care by households without the use of professional healers is common throughout Ethiopia. A popular remedy for different illnesses exists. For instance, remedies for headaches include coffee and lemon tea drinking, and most ethnic groups place eucalyptus leaves in the nostrils to treat colds. Rheumatism and arthritis are treated with an application of hot and dry leaves on the afflicted part of the body, in some population groups. Several skin problems are also treated at home, for example, the Sidamo applies a poultice derived from butter and leaves to scabies-caused burrows.

Empirical Practitioners

Beyond the self-care practices, Ethiopians use a different variety of traditional medical practitioners, who operate predominantly at an empirical level. Group-specific taxonomic terms distinguish further ethno medical competence. Thus, a Sidamo traditional medical practitioner whose field of expertise is restricted solely to the preparation of herbal concoctions is designated with the term "Taghissancho", meaning medicine maker. The Amhara also classify the traditional medical practitioners as herbalists, "Wegesha" (bonesetter), uvula cutter, and cupper. These people are not distinguishable from the rest of the population in terms of social status or insignia. The majority of them are engaged in farming and practice medicine on a part-time basis.

Cauterization

Cauterization is a popular medical practice in Ethiopia and is advised for ailments such as conjunctivitis, headaches, ear infections, chronic cough, and bone fracture. Although cautery is rarely harmful, cases of permanent disability following cauterization were observed among the Sidamo. The attributed efficacy of cautery is based on the belief that the emanation of heat destroys the pathogenic substance inside the affected part of the body.

Surgery

Though rare, literatures report the practices of tonsillectomy median episiotomies, amputation, and caesarian section. In Ethiopia presently the most common procedures that entail the excision of an anatomical part are Circumcisions and Uvulectomy.

Miscellaneous practices

Additional ethno medical procedures include bathing, bone setting and cupping. Thermal springs have traditionally been important in Ethiopia in treating skin diseases, syphilis, leprosy, rheumatism, and other ailments. Segregation of highly contagious patients is generally enforced, especially in case of leprosy. Bone setting techniques vary among ethnic groups.

Traditional practitioners treat bone fractures, dislocation and sprains.

Therapeutic cupping

Therapeutic cupping is practiced alongside other bleeding techniques. Its main objective is to extract "bad blood" from the body, which is thought to be decaying internally causing tissue swelling and ill health. It is prescribed for elephantiasis, rheumatism, high fevers, headaches and others. Additional ethno medical practices include dentistry involving the use of modern carpenter pliers to extract aching teeth, eye, and brow cutting to treat conjunctivitis, and scrapping the buccal tissue in the case of tonsillitis.

IV

Health and Community Developments

Introduction

Individuals in good health are better able to study, learn and be more productive in their work. Improvements in the standard of living have long been known to contribute to improved public health; however, the course has not always been recognized. Investment in health care was not considered a high priority in many countries where economic considerations directed investment to the "productive" sectors such as manufacturing and large scale infrastructure projects, such as hydroelectric dams. The socially-oriented approach observes investment in health as necessary for the protection and development of "human capital" just as investment in education is needed for the long-term benefit of the economy of a country.

The World Development Report by World Bank in1993: Investing in health, articulated a new approach to economic growth in which health, along with education and social development are considered essential contributors to economic development. Development on the other hand should be the concern of all in the developing countries. The health planner, manager, and others are equally charged with that concern and must be knowledgeable of what development implies and the role health should play in the development of one's country.

Hence, it is important to know what development means, how does it differ from economic growth? What role does health play in development? What is development? Development has been variously defined. The modern view of development perceives it as both a physical reality and a state of mind in which society has, through some combination of social, economic and institutional processes, secured the means for obtaining a better life.

Development in all societies must consist of at least the following:

To increase the availability, distribution and accessibility of life sustaining goods such as food, shelter, health, security and protection to all members of society.

To raise standards of living including higher incomes, the provision of more jobs, better education and better health and more attention to cultural and humanistic values so as to enhance not only material well-being, but also to generate greater individual, community and national esteem.

To expand the range of economic and social opportunities and services to individuals and communities by freeing them from servitude and dependence on other people and communities and from ignorance and human misery.

Difference between development and Economic growth

For a long time, the terms development and economic growth were used interchangeably. Although the two are closely related, they are, however, different. Development encompasses the total well-being of individual, a community or a nation. Must be measured by the rate of economic growth Concerned with the total person, his economic, social, political, physiological, and psychic and environmental requirements. Economic growth can be defined as an increase in a country's productive capacity, identifiable by a sustained rise in real national income over a period of years.

Concerned with the area in per capita earnings of the people making up the nation. To depict one characteristic of development It may be possible for a county to experience economic growth without development.

Role of health sector in development

Health plays a major role in promoting economic development and reducing poverty. The health sector is the key social sector for development. Good health, both at the individual, community and national levels, is a prerequisite for full-scale productivity and creativity. In the first place, the health sector should not be looked at in isolation from the rest of the economy, as a sort of charitable handout to ensure that people do not die, for example, of preventive diseases. The development of the health sector is seen to be a necessary requirement for future development.

The fact that development in the health sector may lead to further general development has given rise to a new area of economic theory called "Investment in Human Capital". The importance of this theory is that it not only helps to explain the development process in an economic way, but it also forms the basis for measuring benefit in cost benefit-analysis in the health sector. This is not to suggest that all the benefit of health or education projects is necessarily economic.

Development is linked not just to the improvement of social indicators or the attainment of basic needs, but to wider aspirations such as high health status, and social well-being and change. The development process embraces not only the so-called "productive" sectors of the economy, but also the social sectors. Health sector, besides producing benefits, which in their own right are necessary for improving the wellbeing of the people, development of the health sector helps to lay the foundation for development in the wider sense. Improving human's capacity to produce more and to fulfill theses needs and aspirations does this.

Relationship between Health and Development

Health development is an important element in the overall development of a country. For instance, in countries where HIV/AIDS is a public health problem, there is a great challenge in getting skilled human power and the country will get a burden in the health delivery by spending the significant figure of the health budget on the pandemic. Here HIV/AIDS is not only a health problem but also a situation that brings social, economic and political crises to a country. In a country with a greater proportion of its people still struggling for their daily survival, the scope of development definition shall fit to the local scenarios. It has to be understood in terms of household Livelihood security.

Household Livelihood Security (HLS)

Household Livelihood Security is defined as: 'Adequate and Sustainable Access to Income and Resources to Meet Basic Needs', including: Food, Proper Nutrition, Clean Water; Health, Health Facilities and services; Economic Opportunities; Education; Housing/Habitat Security; Physical Safety; and time for Community Participation. A system in which there are activities that households engage in to earn/make a living, which can consist of a range of on- and off-farm activities or procurement strategies together, provides food and/or cash. The assets & other resources that households possess and the human and social capital that households possess or can call on in times of need.

The livelihood systems of the poor are often quite diverse. Households often use their capabilities, skills, and know-how to diversify income sources and offset risks. It can be said livelihood is secured, when households have secure ownership of, or access to, resources and income-earning opportunities. This includes reserves and assets to: offset risks, ease shocks, and meet contingencies. The common factors or situations (risks or shocks) that lead to livelihood insecurity include Drought and Floods, Conflict, Disease outbreaks & illness, Population growth, Economic adjustment policies, Natural resource degradation, etc. As it is described above livelihood, security is 'Adequate and sustainable access to income and resources to meet basic needs (one of which is health)'.

This means Health is a basic commodity of livelihood; it is an important means as well as the the prerequisite for achieving livelihood security. The three key linked and interrelated issues that justify such mechanism, are: first, the important relation of health with access to income and other resources which are core to livelihood; second, any risk or shock of any cause are manifested in terms of health problems; and finally, health and health-related problems (disease outbreaks & illness, population growth, etc) are among the key factors (risks or shocks) that lead to livelihood insecurity. All these three mechanisms affect the livelihood security via affecting level of productivity; income, savings and expenditures (key determinateness of access); utilization and distribution of resources. Good health affects several aspects of life and personal well-being. A healthy population will have high work productivity, and thereby contribute to the improvement of country's living standards.

A healthy population may also require less health care, which implies lower health expenditures for both the individual and the public sector. Poor health on the other hand, make people unable to work full-time and thus their income level is reduced which will affect their livelihood and they will not be able to get their basic needs including health services. Hence, the relationship of health status and income is like the 'chicken and egg dilemma' and is bi-direction. This effect is reflected at the individual level, household and community level.

Health and health-related problems affect household access to income, economic growth, and resource distribution resulting in challenged household livelihood security and resilience. Ill health not only affects the means (financial resources, assets, income, know-how, time, etc,) to livelihood but also modifies or complicates the context such as the economic, cultural, political and social situations in which individuals making effort to achieve their livelihood basic needs. Thus, in order to have a better livelihood, families should be economically secured. Economic security is achieved when individuals or households have the capacity to generate sufficient income to satisfy the basic needs of the family, and to maintain or increase the goods necessary for the stability of the family economy, as well as to protect it against shocks. As a prerequisite for this, households should have health security and should be nutritionally secured.

Health and the Millennium Development Goal

During September 2000, leaders of 191 countries around the world met at the UN to adopt the Millennium Declaration. The Declaration outlined the central concerns of the global community and articulated a set of interconnected and mutually reinforcing goals for sustainable development that are now designated as the Millennium Development Goals (MDGs). The MDGs, as set of global development agendas reflect the renewed commitment of the international community toward the overall well-being of people in the developing world. Political and economic externality issues aside, the altruistic rationale behind the MDGs within the health sector can be considered as paralleling the philanthropic drives of the 1970s that led to the emergence of the "Health For All by 2000" movement.

The eight major goals of the MDGs, most of which are to be achieved by the year 2015, are:

1. Eradication of extreme poverty and hunger
2. Achievement of universal primary education
3. Promotion of gender equality and empowerment of women
4. Reduction of child mortality
5. Improvement in maternal health
6. Combating HIV/AIDS, malaria and other diseases
7. Ensuring environmental sustainability
8. Developing a global partnership for development.

V

Public Health Concerns for Geriatric People

Definitions

How old is old? A person's age might depend upon who measures it and how they define it. For example, while demographers might define old according to chronological years, clinicians might define it by stages of physiological development, and psychologists by developmental stages. Children might see their 35-year-old teacher as old, while the 35-year-old teacher might regard her 61-year-old principal as old. Age is and always will be a relative concept.

In developed and developing countries, people are considered old once they reach the age of 65. But because there are a number of people who are very active and healthy at age 65 and will live a number of productive years after 65, researchers have subdivided the old into the young-old (65–74), the older old (75 and over), and the oldest old (85 and over). Interestingly enough, it is this latter group, the oldest old, that makes up the fastest-growing segment of the elder population. Mihir Bhatta and his co-workers had chosen men and women of the age of more than 55 years as the geriatric people, in their research on HIV care for Geriatric people.

Myths Surrounding Aging

Like other forms of prejudice and discrimination, ageism is the result of ignorance, misconceptions, and half-truths about aging and the elderly. Because most people do not interact with older people on a daily basis, it is easy to create a stereotypical image of elders based upon the atypical actions of a few. When you think of older people, who comes to mind? Do you immediately think of a lonely man with a dishevelled appearance sitting on a park bench or an older person lying in bed in a nursing home making incomprehensible noises?

Demography of Aging

Demography is "the study of a population (an aggregate of individuals) and those variables bringing about change in that population." The demography of aging is typically defined as a study of those who are 65 years and over and of the variables that bring about change in their lives. In the following paragraphs, we review some of the demographic features of the elder population, including size, growth rate, and the factors that contribute to this growth. We also discuss other demographic characteristics of this population, such as living arrangements, racial and ethnic composition, geographic distribution, economic status, and housing.

Potential Roles in Healthy Aging

Public health needs to be a critical partner in all efforts to support and promote programs that improve the health and well-being of older adults. Evidence shows that disease prevention and health promotion programs are effective, and they are the domain of public health (Keck School of Medicine). Throughout the 20th century, public health played a crucial role in adding years to life. In the 21st century, public health can play a crucial role in adding life to years. Recognizing the significant role the U.S. public health system can play in strengthening older adult health, Trust for America's Health (TFAH) led a convening in 2017, funded by The John A. Hartford Foundation, to explore potential roles for public health in healthy aging. National, state, and local public health officials, aging experts, advocates, service providers, and health care officials who participated in the convening strongly endorsed a greater role for public health in aging. Through an examination of case studies of older adults, participants identified gaps in services, supports, and policies needed to improve older adult health and well-being and considered the potential roles public health could play in filling these identified gaps. The resulting Framework for an Age-Friendly Public Health System outlines the functions that public health could fulfil, in collaboration with aging services and the health care sector to address the challenges and opportunities of an aging society. The main takeaway from the convening was the need for an Age-Friendly Public Health (AFPH) system that recognizes aging as a core public health issue.

Healthy aging is defined in the Framework as (i) promoting health, preventing disease, injury, and frailty, and managing chronic conditions; (ii) optimizing physical, cognitive, and mental health; and (iii) facilitating social and civic engagement. This definition intentionally does not equate healthy aging with the absence of disease and disability. Instead, it portrays healthy aging as both an adaptive process in response to the challenges that can occur as we age, and a proactive process to reduce the likelihood, intensity, or impact of future challenges. Healthy aging involves maximizing physical, mental, emotional, and social well-being, while recognizing that aging is often accompanied by chronic illnesses and functional limitations. It also emphasizes the importance of meaningful involvement of older adults with others, such as friends, family members, neighbours, organizations, and the wider community. Although the public health sector has experience and skill in addressing these components of health for some populations, it has not traditionally focused attention on older adults.

The Framework is not a prescriptive guide to action or a declaration of the public health sector's oversight of certain activities. Not every community will need public health to assume each of these roles. Agencies and organizations in other sectors are already actively engaged in healthy aging but are not leveraging the expertise of public health professionals. Public health should work in partnership with these organizations to promote healthy aging. Furthermore, public health organizations lack the resources to focus on healthy aging and will thus need to carefully and thoughtfully prioritize their roles. The Framework offers a useful articulation of the potential contributions that public health should consider as it embraces a larger role in optimizing the health of older adults.

To explore these functions more fully through actual public health experience, TFAH initiated the Florida-based Age-Friendly Public Health

Learning and Action Network (AFPH Network), with funding from The John A. Hartford Foundation. TFAH created an application process to select county health departments (CHDs) to participate in the AFPH Network and conducted interviews with all prospective county teams. With support from the Florida Departments of Health and Elder Affairs, all applicants were invited to participate. The AFPH Network includes teams from 37 of Florida's 67 CHDs, representing 65% of Florida's overall population and 65% of the older adult population.

Impairments

Impairments are deficits in the functioning of one's sense organs or limitations in one's mobility or range of motion. Like chronic conditions, impairments are far more prevalent in older elders. The four primary impairments are hearing impairments, orthopaedic impairments, cataracts, and other visual impairments. Another impairment of great concern is memory impairment. "Memory skills are important to general cognitive functioning, declining scores on tests of memory are indicators of general cognitive loss for older adults. Low cognitive functioning (i.e. memory impairment) is a major risk factor for entering a nursing home." Like rates for chronic conditions, rates for impairments differ by gender and race. But unlike chronic conditions, impairments are affected by two other variables—previous income level and previous occupational exposure. The smaller the income and the more occupational exposure to health hazards, the greater the number of impairments.

Elder abuse and neglect

Incidents of elder abuse and neglect have increased greatly in recent years. During ten years, reports of elder abuse increased by more than 200%. Perhaps a substantial part of the increase in these numbers was due to an increase in communication and the apt role of media. Though the laws and definitions of terms vary from state to state, all states have set up reporting systems. Prior to the reporting systems, many incidences of abuse were never recorded.

According to the first-ever National Elder Abuse Incidence Study in USA, in 1998, an estimated total of 551,000 elderly persons over the age of 60 had experienced abuse (physical, emotional/psychological), neglect, or self-neglect in a domestic setting during the years.

It was also revealed that:

- Female elders are abused at a higher rate than men.
- Elders 80 years and older are abused or neglected at two to three times the rate of their proportion of the elderly population.
- In almost 90% of all elder abuse and neglect incidents where a perpetrator is identified, the perpetrator is a family member, and two-thirds of the perpetrators are adult children or spouses.
- Victims of self-neglect are usually depressed, confused, or extremely frail.

Elder abuse and neglect are special problems for elders because they are (1) frail, (2) unable to defend themselves, (3) vulnerable to telemarketing scams and mail-order swindles, and (4) the most common victims of theft of their benefit checks. But on a positive note, elder abuse is a problem that has responded well to community health programming.

Needs of elder people

There are six instrumental needs that determine lifestyles for people of all age viz. income, housing, personal care, health care, transportation, community facilities and services. However, the aging process can alter these needs in unpredictable ways. While those elders in the young-old group (65–74) usually do not experience appreciable changes in their lifestyles relative to these six needs, elders in the older old group (75–84) and the oldest old group (85 and older) eventually do.

Income

Though the need for income continues throughout one's life, achieving elder status often reduces the income needs. Perhaps the major reduction occurs with one's retirement. Retirees do not need to purchase job-related items such as special clothing or tools, pay union dues, or join professional associations. Expenses are further reduced because retirees no longer commute every day, buy as many meals away from home, or spend money on business travel. Reaching elder status also usually means that children are grown and no longer dependent, and, as noted earlier, the home mortgage has often been retired. Taxes are usually lower because income is lower. In addition, many community services are offered at reduced prices for elders. However, aging usually means increased expenses for health care and for home maintenance and repairs that aging homeowners can no longer do themselves. In spite of these increased costs, the overall need for income seems to decrease slightly for people after retirement.

Housing

Housing, a basic necessity for all, is a central concern for elders in terms of needs and costs. It is an important source of continuity for elders. A home is more than just a place to live. It is a symbol of independence; a place for family gatherings; a source of pleasant memories; and a link to friends, the neighborhood, and the community. When housing for the elderly is examined, four major needs are discussed. They include appropriateness, accessibility, adequacy, and affordability.

These needs are not independent of each other; in fact, they are closely intertwined. Elders may live in affordable housing, but the housing may not be appropriate for their special needs. Or, certain housing may be accessible to the elderly, but it may not be affordable to elders, or there may not be an adequate number available to meet demand. Housing requirements may change more rapidly than housing consumption during the course of retirement years as a result of changes in household composition, decreasing mobility, and/or increasing morbidity. Thus, the single biggest change in the housing needs of elders is the need for special modifications due to physical disabilities. Such modifications can be very simple—such as handrails for support in bathrooms—or more complex—such as chair lifts for stairs. Sometimes there is need for live-in help, while at other times disabilities may force seniors to leave their homes and seek specialized housing.

Personal Care

While most elders are able to care for themselves, there is a significant minority of elders who require personal assistance for an optimal or even adequate existence. The size of this minority increases as the elders attain older old (75–84) and oldest old (85) status.

When elders begin to need help with one or more of these tasks, it is usually a spouse, adult children, or other family members who first provide the help, thus assuming the role of informal caregivers. An informal caregiver has been defined as one who provides unpaid care or assistance to one who has some physical, mental, emotional, or financial need that limits his or her independence. The need for personal care for elders is projected to increase in the coming years. The primary responsibility for providing and financing this care will fall on the family. Due to the financial burden, more families will begin purchasing long-term health care insurance policies. These policies are very expensive if purchased after age 75 but do provide elders with sufficient income protection against the depletion of assets.

Caregivers for elders face a number of problems, including decreased personal freedom, lack of privacy, constant demands on their time and energy, resentment that siblings do not share in the caregiving, and an increased financial burden. Many experience feelings of guilt for asking a spouse to help with the care of an in-law, or in knowing that the end of caregiving responsibilities usually means either the elder person's death or placement in a group home. Caregivers often experience a change in lifestyle, especially associated with time for leisure and recreation.

Health Care

Health care is a major issue for all segments of our society, particularly for elders. While significant progress has been made in extending life expectancy, a longer life does not necessarily mean a healthier life. Health problems naturally increase with age. With these problems comes a need for increased health care services. All indications are that the health care costs for elders will continue to escalate because of the aging population and rising health care costs. Future legislators will be forced to choose from among the following alternatives:

1. Raising taxes to pay for the care.
2. Reallocating tax dollars from other programs to pay for care.
3. Cutting back on coverage presently offered.
4. Offering care to only those who truly cannot afford it otherwise (also known as means testing) and

5. Completely revamping the present system under which the care is funded.

In the meantime, the importance of instilling in Americans the value of preventing the onset of chronic diseases through healthy living cannot be overstated. While it is not possible to prevent all chronic health problems, encouraging healthy behaviours is a step in the right direction.

Transportation

Transportation is of prime importance to elders because it enables them to remain independent. Housing, medical, financial and social services are useful only to the extent that transportation can make them accessible to those in need. With regard to transportation needs, elders can be categorized into three different groups as follows:

1. Elder people, who can use the present forms of transportation, whether it be their own vehicle or public transportation.
2. Those who could use public transportation if the barriers of cost and access (no service available) were removed, and
3. Elders, who need special services (that it may be a vehicle that can accommodate a wheelchair) beyond what is available through public transportation.

While these services have been helpful to elders, mobility is still more difficult for elders than for other adults.

Community Facilities and Services

As has been mentioned previously, one of the most common occurrences of the aging process is loss of independence. Even some of the most basic activities of adults become major tasks for elders because of low income, ill health, and lack of transportation. Because of the limitations of elders and the barriers they must face, they have special needs in regard to community facilities and services. If these needs are met, the lifestyles of elders are greatly enhanced. If not, they are confronted with anything from a slight inconvenience to a very poor quality of life.

VI

Addiction and Community Health

Introduction

Addiction to any narcotics eventually compromises community health. Here, we will discuss the addiction and addiction related public health concerns of alcohol, tobacco, and other drugs by defining some terms. A drug is a substance, other than food or vitamins that upon entering the body in small amounts alters one's physical, mental, or emotional state. Psychoactive drugs are drugs that alter sensory perceptions, mood, thought processes, or behaviours.

Drug use is a non-evaluative term referring to drug-taking behaviour in general, regardless of whether the behaviour is appropriate. Drug misuse refers primarily to the inappropriate use of legally purchased prescription or non-prescription drugs. For example, drug misuse occurs when one discontinues the use of a prescribed antibiotic before the entire prescribed dose is completed or when one takes four aspirin rather than two as specified on the label.

Drug abuse can be defined in several ways depending upon the drug and the situation. Drug abuse occurs when one takes a prescription or non-prescription drug for a purpose other than that for which it is medically approved. For example, drug abuse occurs when one takes a prescription diet pill for its mood altering effects (stimulation).

The abuse of legal drugs such as nicotine or alcohol is said to occur when one is aware that continued use is detrimental to one's health. Because illicit drugs have no approved medical uses, any illicit drug use is considered drug abuse. Likewise, the use of alcohol and nicotine by those under the legal age is considered drug abuse. Drug (chemical) dependence occurs when a user feels that a particular drug is necessary for normal functioning.

Dependence may be psychological, in which case the user experiences a strong emotional or psychological desire to continue use of the drug even though clinical signs of physical illness may not appear; or it can be physical, in which discontinuation of drug use results in clinical illness. Usually, both psychological and physical dependence are present at the same time, making the discontinuation of drug use results in clinical illness. Usually, both psychological and physical dependence are present at the same time, making the discontinuation of drug use is very difficult. Such is frequently the case with cigarette smoking.

Risk and protective factors can be either genetic (inherited) or environmental. Numerous studies have concluded that inherited traits can increase one's risk of developing dependence on alcohol, and it is logical to assume that susceptibility to other drugs might also be inherited. Environmental risk factors, such as one's home and family life, school and peer groups, and society and culture have also been identified.

Personal Factors

Personal factors include personality traits, such as impulsiveness, depressive mood, susceptibility to stress, or possibly personality disturbances. It is difficult to determine the degree to which these factors are inherited or are simply the product of the family environment. For example, one's choice to use alcohol or drugs in response to a stressful situation (and the outcome of that decision) could be the result of either inherited characteristics, learned behaviour, or a combination of these factors.

Family and surroundings

The development of interpersonal skills, such as communication skills, independent living skills, and learning to get along with others, is nurtured in the home. The failure of parents to provide an environment conducive to the development of these skills can result in the loss of self-esteem and increase in delinquency, nonconformity, and sociopathic behaviour, all personal risk factors for alcohol and drug abuse. Parent's attitudes toward alcohol and drug uses influence adolescents' beliefs and expectations about the effects of drugs. These expectations have been shown to be important factors in adolescents' choices to initiate and continue alcohol use. The age of first use of alcohol, tobacco, and illicit drugs is correlated to later development of alcohol and drug problems, especially if use begins before age of adolescent.

School and Peer Groups

Perceived and actual drug use by peers influences attitudes and choices by adolescents). Some studies have shown that perceived support of drinking by peers is the single most important factor in an adolescent's choice to drink. Peers can also influence expectations for a drug. Alcohol may be perceived as "a 'magic elixir' that can enhance social and physical pleasure, sexual performance and responsiveness, power and aggression and social competence." It is interesting to note that these are precisely the mythical qualities about alcohol portrayed in advertisements for beer and other alcoholic beverages.

Drug Abuse: Prevention and Control

Prevention and control of alcohol and other drug abuse require knowledge of the causes of drug-taking behaviour, sources of illicit drugs, drug laws, and treatment programs. Also required are community organizing skills, persistence, and cooperation among a vast array of concerned individuals and governmental and non-governmental agencies.

Levels of Prevention

Drug abuse prevention activities can be viewed as primary, secondary, or tertiary depending upon the point of intervention.

Primary prevention programs are aimed at those who have never used drugs, and their goal is to prevent or forestall the initiation of drug use. Drug education programs that stress primary prevention of drug and alcohol use are most appropriate and successful for children at the elementary school age. In a broader sense, almost any activity that would reduce the likelihood of primary drug use could be considered primary prevention. For example, raising the price of alcohol, increasing cigarette taxes, arresting a neighbourhood drug pusher, or destroying a cocaine crop in Bolivia could be considered primary prevention if it forestalled primary drug use in at least some individuals.

Secondary prevention programs are aimed at those who have begun alcohol or other drug use but who have not become chronic abusers and have not suffered significant physical or mental impairment from their drug or alcohol abuse. Alcohol and other drug abuse education programs that stress secondary prevention are often appropriate for people of high school or college age. They can be presented in educational, workplace, or community settings.

Tertiary prevention programs are designed to provide drug abuse treatment and aftercare, including relapse prevention programs. As such, they are usually designed for adults. Tertiary programs for teenagers are far too uncommon. Tertiary prevention programs may receive clients who "turn themselves in" for treatment voluntarily, but more often than not their clients are referred by the courts.

Elements of Prevention

Education

The purpose of drug abuse education is to limit the demand for drugs by providing information about drugs and the dangers of drug abuse, changing attitudes and beliefs about drugs, providing the skills necessary to abstain from drugs, and ultimately changing drug abuse behaviour. Education, principally a primary prevention activity, can be school-based or community-based. A school based program programs must be supported by parents, teachers, local business people, and others community members.

Treatment

The goal of treatment is to remove the physical, emotional, and environmental conditions that have contributed to drug dependency. Like education, treatment aims to reduce demand for drugs. It also aims to save money. Treatment for drug abuse occurs in a variety of settings and involves a variety of approaches. Treatment may be residential (inpatient) or non-residential (outpatient). Under managed care, "behavioural health care" guidelines usually limit inpatient care to 28 days, after which the care may continue on an outpatient basis. In drug abuse treatment, what happens after the initial treatment phase is critical. Aftercare, the continuing care provided the recovering former drug abuser, often involves peer group or self-help support group meetings, such as those provided by Alcoholics Anonymous (AA) or Narcotics Anonymous (NA). Despite frequent relapses, treatment for drug dependence is viewed as an important component of a community's comprehensive drug abuse prevention and control strategy.

Public Policy

Public policy embodies the guiding principles and courses of action pursued by governments to solve practical problems affecting society. Examples include passing drunk-driving laws or zoning ordinances that limit the number of bars in a neighbourhood and enacting ordinances that regulate the type and amount of advertising for such legal drugs as alcohol and tobacco. Public policy should guide the budget discussions that ultimately determine how much a community spends for education, treatment, and law enforcement. Further examples of public policy decisions are restrictions of smoking in public buildings, the setting of 0.08% blood alcohol concentration as the point at which driving becomes illegal, and zero tolerance laws for BACs for minors. Setting the level of state excise taxes on alcohol and tobacco is also a public policy decision.

Application of law

Law enforcement in drug abuse prevention and control is the application of central, federal, state, and local laws to arrest, jail, bring to trial, and sentence those who break laws because of drug use. The primary roles of law enforcement in a drug abuse prevention and control program are to control drug use, control crime, especially crime related to drug use and drug trafficking—the buying, selling, manufacturing, or transporting of illegal drugs, prevent the establishment of crime organizations, and protect neighbourhoods. Law enforcement is concerned with limiting the supply of drugs in the community by interrupting the source, transit, and distribution of drugs.

VII

Pollution: A Public Health Concern

Air Pollution

Until a few hundred years ago, air pollution could be attributed almost entirely to natural causes—dust and sand storms, forest fires, volcanic eruptions, and the gases escaping from deep within the earth or given off by decaying organic matter. While these forms of air pollution still exist today, waste products created by a modern industrialized civilization constitute a greater threat to air quality and our health.

Air pollution by anthropogenic activities:

Carbon dioxide (CO_2): Because of its role as a greenhouse gas it has been described as "the leading pollutant" and "the worst climate pollutant". Carbon dioxide is a natural component of the atmosphere, essential for plant life and given off by the human respiratory system. This question of terminology has practical effects, for example as determining whether the U.S. Clean Air Act is deemed to regulate CO_2 emissions. CO_2 currently forms about 410 parts per million (ppm) of earth's atmosphere, compared to about 280 ppm in pre-industrial times, and billions of metric tons of CO_2 are emitted annually by burning of fossil fuels. CO_2 increase in earth's atmosphere has been accelerating.

Sulphur oxides (SOx): particularly sulphur dioxide, a chemical compound with the formula SO_2. SO_2 is produced by volcanoes and in various industrial processes. Coal and petroleum often contain sulphur compounds, and their combustion generates sulphur dioxide. Further oxidation of SO_2, usually in the presence of a catalyst such as NO_2, forms H_2SO_4, and thus acid rain is formed. This is one of the causes for concern over the environmental impact of the use of these fuels as power sources.

Nitrogen oxides (NOx): Nitrogen oxides, particularly nitrogen dioxide, are expelled from high temperature combustion, and are also produced during thunderstorms by electric discharge. They can be seen as a brown haze dome above or a plume downwind of cities. Nitrogen dioxide is a chemical compound with the formula NO2. It is one of several nitrogen oxides. One of the most prominent air pollutants, this reddish-brown toxic gas has a characteristic sharp, biting odour.

Carbon monoxide (CO): CO is a colourless, odourless, toxic gas. It is a product of combustion of fuel such as natural gas, coal or wood. Vehicular exhaust contributes to the majority of carbon monoxide let into the atmosphere. It creates a smog type formation in the air that has been linked to many lung diseases and disruptions to the natural environment and animals.

Volatile organic compounds (VOC): VOCs are a well-known outdoor air pollutant. They are categorized as either methane (CH4) or non-methane (NMVOCs). Methane is an extremely efficient greenhouse gas which contributes to enhance global warming. Other hydrocarbon VOCs are also significant greenhouse gases because of their role in creating ozone and prolonging the life of methane in the atmosphere. This effect varies depending on local air quality. The aromatic NMVOCs benzene, toluene and xylene are suspected carcinogens and may lead to leukaemia with prolonged exposure. 1, 3-butadiene is another dangerous compound often associated with industrial use.

Particulate matter/particles, also known as particulate matter (PM), atmospheric particulate matter (APM), or fine particles, are microscopic solid or liquid particles suspended in a gas. Aerosol, on the other hand, is a mixture of particles and gas. Volcanoes, dust storms, forest and grassland fires, living plants, and sea spray are all sources of particles. Aerosols are produced by human activities such as the combustion of fossil fuels in automobiles, power plants, and numerous industrial processes. Averaged worldwide, anthropogenic aerosols – those made by human activities – currently account for approximately 10% of our atmosphere. Increased levels of fine particles in the air are linked to health hazards such as heart disease, altered lung function and lung cancer. Particulates are related to respiratory infections and can be particularly harmful to those with conditions like asthma. Persistent free radicals connected to airborne fine particles are linked to cardiopulmonary disease. Toxic metals, such as lead and mercury, especially their compounds.

Chlorofluorocarbons (CFCs): Emitted from goods that are now prohibited from use; harmful to the ozone layer. These are gases emitted by air conditioners, freezers, aerosol sprays, and other similar devices. CFCs reach the stratosphere after being released into the atmosphere. They interact with other gases here, causing harm to the ozone layer. UV rays are able to reach the earth's surface as a result of this. This can result in skin cancer, eye problems, and even plant damage.

Ammonia: Emitted mainly by agricultural waste. Ammonia is a compound with the formula NH3. It is normally encountered as a gas with a characteristic pungent odour. Ammonia contributes significantly to the nutritional needs of terrestrial organisms by serving as a precursor to foodstuffs and fertilizers. Ammonia, either directly or indirectly, is also a building block for the synthesis of many pharmaceuticals. Although in wide use, ammonia is both caustic and hazardous. In the atmosphere, ammonia reacts with oxides of nitrogen and sulphur to form secondary particles.

Odours: Such as from garbage, sewage, and industrial processes.

Radioactive pollutants: Produced by nuclear explosions, nuclear events, war explosives, and natural processes such as the radioactive decay of radon.

Secondary pollutants include:

Photochemical smog: particles are formed from gaseous primary contaminants and chemicals. Smog is a type of pollution that occurs in the atmosphere. Smog is caused by a huge volume of coal being burned in a certain region, resulting in a mixture of smoke and sulphur dioxide. Modern smog is usually caused by automotive and industrial emissions, which are acted on in the atmosphere by UV light from the sun to produce secondary pollutants, which then combine with the primary emissions to generate photochemical smog.

Ground level ozone (O3): Ozone is created when NOx and VOCs mix. It is a significant part of the troposphere. It's also an important part of the ozone layer, which can be found in different sections of the stratosphere.

Photochemical and chemical reactions involving it fuel many of the chemical activities that occur in the atmosphere during the day and night. It is a pollutant and a component of smog that is produced in large quantities as a result of human activities (mostly the combustion of fossil fuels).

Peroxyacetyl nitrate ($C_2H_3NO_5$): similarly formed from NOx and VOCs.

Minor air pollutants include:

A large number of minor hazardous air pollutants. Some of these are regulated in USA under the Clean Air Act and in Europe under the Air Framework Directive. A variety of persistent organic pollutants, which can attach to particulates. Persistent organic pollutants are organic compounds that are resistant to environmental degradation due to chemical, biological, or photolytic processes (POPs). As a result, they've been discovered to survive in the environment, be capable of long-range transmission, bio-accumulate in human and animal tissue, bio-magnify in food chains, and pose a major threat to human health and the ecosystem.

Noise pollution

Noise pollution, also known as environmental noise or sound pollution, is the propagation of noise with ranging impacts on the activity of human or animal life, most of them harmful to a degree. The source of outdoor noise worldwide is mainly caused by machines, transport, and propagation systems. Poor urban planning may give rise to noise disintegration or pollution, side-by-side industrial and residential buildings can result in noise pollution in the residential areas. Some of the main sources of noise in residential areas include loud music, transportation (traffic, rail, airplanes, etc.), lawn care maintenance, construction, electrical generators, wind turbines, explosions, and people.

Documented problems associated with noise in urban environments go back as far as ancient Rome. Today, the average noise level of 98 decibels (dB) exceeds the WHO value of 50 dB allowed for residential areas. Research suggests that noise pollution in the United States is the highest in low-income and racial minority neighbourhoods, and noise pollution associated with household electricity generators is an emerging environmental degradation in many developing nations. High noise levels can contribute to cardiovascular effects in humans and an increased incidence of coronary artery disease. In animals, noise can increase the risk of death by altering predator or prey detection and avoidance, interfere with reproduction and navigation, and contribute to permanent hearing loss. A substantial amount of the noise that humans produce occurs in the ocean. Up until recently, most research on noise impacts has been focused on marine mammals, and to a lesser degree, fish.

In the past few years, scientists have shifted to conducting studies on invertebrates and their responses to anthropogenic sounds in the marine environment. This research is essential, especially considering that invertebrates make up 75% of marine species, and thus compose a large percentage of ocean food webs. Among the studies that have been conducted, a sizable variety in families of invertebrates have been represented in the research. A variation in the complexity of their sensory systems exists, which allows scientists to study a range of characteristics and develop a better understanding of anthropogenic noise impacts on living organisms.

Effects on human health

Cardiovascular health problems

Noise has been associated with important cardiovascular health problems, particularly hypertension, as it causes an increase in levels of stress hormones and vascular oxidative stress. Noise levels of 50 dB(A) or greater at night may increase the risk of myocardial infarction by chronically elevating cortisol production.

Traffic noise has several negative effects, including increased risk for coronary artery disease, with night-time exposure to noise possibly more harmful than day-time exposure. It has also been shown to increase blood pressure in individuals within the surrounding residential areas, with railways causing the greatest cardiovascular effects. Roadway noise levels are sufficient to constrict arterial blood flow and lead to elevated blood pressure. Vasoconstriction can result from elevated adrenaline levels or through medical stress reactions. Long-term exposure to noise is correlated to increase in cortisol and angiotensin-II levels which are respectively associated with oxidative stress and vascular inflammation. Individuals subject to great than 80 dB(A) in the workplace are at increased risk of having increased blood pressure.

A 2021 systematic review on the effect of occupational exposure to noise on ischaemic heart disease (IHD), stroke and hypertension, coordinated by the World Health Organization (WHO) and the International Labour Organization (ILO) located 17 studies that met the inclusion criteria, comprising a total of 534,688 participants (7.47% females) in 11 countries and in three WHO regions (the Americas, Europe, and the Western Pacific). The study found the low quality of evidence the effect of occupational exposure to intense noise (≥85 dBA), compared to occupational exposure below 85 dBA (<85 dBA). They concluded that there is an inadequate evidence of harmfulness for the studied outcomes with the exception for the risk of acquiring IHD, which was 29% higher for those exposed to noise in their workplace. Because the local civic noise environment can impact the perceived value of real estate, often the largest equity held by a home owner, personal stakes in the noise environment and the civic politics surrounding the noise environment can run extremely high.

Stress

Researchers are found that in the UK one third (33%) of victims of domestic disturbances claim loud parties have left them unable to sleep or made them stressed in the last two years. Around one in eleven (9%) of those affected by domestic disturbances claims it has left them continually disturbed and stressed. More than 1.8 million people claim noisy neighbours have made their life a misery and they cannot enjoy their own homes. The impact of noise on health is potentially a significant problem across the UK given that more than 17.5 million Britons (38%) have been disturbed by the inhabitants of neighbouring properties in the last two years. For almost one in ten (7%) Britons this is a regular occurrence.

The extent of the problem of noise pollution for public health is reinforced by figures collated by Rockwool from local authority responses to a Freedom of Information Act (FOI) request. This research reveals in the period April 2008 – 2009 UK councils received 315,838 complaints about noise pollution from private residences. This resulted in environmental health officers across the UK serving 8,069 noise abatement notices, or citations under the terms of the Anti-Social Behaviour (Scotland) Act.

Plastic pollution

Plastic pollution is the accumulation of plastic objects and particles (e.g. plastic bottles, bags and microbeads) in the Earth's environment that adversely affects humans, wildlife and their habitat. Plastics that act as pollutants are categorized by size into micro-, meso-, or macro debris. Plastics are inexpensive and durable making them very adaptable for different uses; as a result manufacturers choose to use plastic over other materials. However, the chemical structure of most plastics renders them resistant to many natural processes of degradation and as a result they are slow to degrade. Together, these two factors allow large volumes of plastic to enter the environment as mismanaged waste and for it to persist in the ecosystem.

Plastic pollution can afflict land, waterways and oceans. It is estimated that 1.1 to 8.8 million tonnes of plastic waste enters the ocean from coastal communities each year. It is estimated that there is a stock of 86 million tons of plastic marine debris in the worldwide ocean as of the end of 2013, with an assumption that 1.4% of global plastics produced from 1950 to 2013 has entered the ocean and has accumulated there. Some researchers suggest that by 2050 there could be more plastic than fish in the oceans by weight. Living organisms, particularly marine animals, can be harmed either by mechanical effects such as entanglement in plastic objects, problems related to ingestion of plastic waste, or through exposure to chemicals within plastics that interfere with their physiology. Degraded plastic waste can directly affect humans through both direct consumption (i.e. in tap water), indirect consumption (by eating animals), and disruption of various hormonal mechanisms.

As of 2019, 368 million tonnes of plastic is produced each year; 51% in Asia, where China is the world's largest producer. From the 1950s up to 2018, an estimated 6.3 billion tonnes of plastic has been produced worldwide, of which an estimated 9% has been recycled and another 12% has been incinerated. This large amount of plastic waste enters the environment and causes problems throughout the ecosystem; for example studies suggest that the bodies of 90% of seabirds contain plastic debris. In some areas there have been significant efforts to reduce the prominence of free range plastic pollution, through reducing plastic consumption, litter clean up, and promoting plastic recycling. As of 2020, the global mass of produced plastic exceeds the biomass of all land and marine animals combined. A May 2019 amendment to the Basel Convention regulates the exportation/importation of plastic waste, largely intended to prevent the shipping of plastic waste from developed countries to developing countries. Nearly all countries have joined this agreement. On 2 March 2022 in Nairobi, 175 countries pledged to create a legally binding agreement by the end of the year 2024 with a goal to end plastic pollution.

The amount of plastic waste produced increased during COVID-19 due to increased demand for protective equipment and packaging materials. Higher amounts of plastic ended up in the ocean, especially plastic from medical waste and masks. Several news reports point to a plastic industry trying to take advantage of the health concerns and desire for disposable masks and packaging to increase production of single use plastic.

Effects on humans

Compounds that are used in manufacturing pollute the environment by releasing chemicals into the air and water. Some compounds that are used in plastics, such as phthalates, bisphenol A (BRA), polybrominated diphenyl ether (PBDE), are under close statute and might be very hurtful. Even though these compounds are unsafe, they have been used in the manufacturing of food packaging, medical devices, flooring materials, bottles, perfumes, cosmetics and much more. Inhalation of micro plastics (MPs) have been shown to be one of the major contributors to MP uptake in humans. MPs in the form of dust particles are circulated constantly through ventilation and air conditioning systems indoors. The large dosage of these compounds are hazardous to humans, destroying the endocrine system. BRA imitates the female's hormone called oestrogen. PBD destroys and causes damage to thyroid hormones, which are vital hormone glands that play a major role in the metabolism, growth and development of the human body. MPs can also have a detrimental effect on male reproductive success. MPs such as BPA can interfere with steroid biosynthesis in the male endocrine system and with early stages of spermatogenesis. MPs in men can also create oxidative stress and DNA damage in spermatozoa, causing reduced sperm viability.

Although the level of exposure to these chemicals varies depending on age and geography, most humans experience simultaneous exposure to many of these chemicals. Average levels of daily exposure are below the levels deemed to be unsafe, but more research needs to be done on the effects of low dose exposure on humans. A lot is unknown on how severely humans are physically affected by these chemicals. Some of the chemicals used in plastic production can cause dermatitis upon contact with human skin. In many plastics, these toxic chemicals are only used in trace amounts, but significant testing is often required to ensure that the toxic elements are contained within the plastic by inert material or polymer. Children and women during their reproduction age are at most at risk and more prone to damaging their immune as well as their reproductive system from these hormone-disrupting chemicals. Pregnancy and nursing products such as baby bottles, pacifiers, and plastic feeding utensils place infants and children at a very high risk of exposure.

Human health has also been negatively impacted by plastic pollution. "Almost a third of groundwater sites in the US contain BPA. BPA is harmful at very low concentrations as it interferes with our hormone and reproductive systems. This quote tells us how much of a percentage of our water is contaminated and should not be drunk on a daily basis. "At every stage of its lifecycle, plastic poses distinct risks to human health, arising from both exposure to plastic particles themselves and associated chemicals". This quote is an intro to numerous points of why plastic is damaging to us, such as the carbon that is released when it is being made and transported which is also related to how plastic pollution harms our environment.

A 2022 study published in Environment International found micro plastic in the blood of 80% of people tested in the study, and such micro plastic has the potential to become embedded in human organs.

Clinical significance

Due to the pervasiveness of plastic products, most of the human population is constantly exposed to the chemical components of plastics. In the United States, 95% of adults have had detectable levels of BPA in their urine. Exposure to chemicals such as BPA have been correlated with disruptions in fertility, reproduction, sexual maturation, and other health effects. Specific phthalates have also resulted in similar biological effects.

Thyroid hormone axis

Biphenol A affects gene expression related to the thyroid hormone axis, which affects biological functions such as metabolism and development. BPA can decrease thyroid hormone receptor (TR) activity by increasing TR transcriptional co-repressor activity. This then decreases the level of thyroid hormone binding proteins that bind to triiodothyronine. By affecting the thyroid hormone axis, BPA exposure can lead to hypothyroidism.

Sex hormones

BPA can disrupt normal, physiological levels of sex hormones. It does this by binding to globulins that normally bind to sex hormones such as androgens and oestrogens, leading to the disruption of the balance between the two. BPA can also affect the metabolism or the catabolism of sex hormones. It often acts as an antiandrogen or as an oestrogen, which can cause disruptions in gonadal development and sperm production. Westminster City Council has received more complaints per head of population than any other district in the UK with 9,814 grievances about noise, which equates to 42.32 complaints per thousand residents. Eight of the top 10 councils ranked by complaints per 1,000 residents were in London.

VIII

Application of Statistics in Health

Incidence, Prevalence, and Attack Rates

Three important types of morbidity rates are incidence rates, prevalence rates, and attack rates.

An **incidence rate** is defined as the number of new cases of a disease in a population-at-risk (those in the population who are susceptible to the disease) in a given time period— the number of new cases of influenza in a community over a week's time, for example. Those who became ill with influenza during the previous week and remain ill during the week in question are not counted in an incidence rate. Incidence rates are important in the study of acute diseases, diseases in which the peak severity of symptoms occurs and subsides within days or weeks. These diseases usually move quickly through a population. Examples of acute diseases are the common cold, influenza, chicken pox, measles, and mumps.

Prevalence rates are calculated by dividing all current cases of a disease (old and new) by the total population. Prevalence rates are useful for the study of chronic diseases, diseases that usually last three months or longer. In these cases, it is more important to know how many people are currently suffering from a chronic disease—such as arthritis, heart disease, cancer, or diabetes—than it is to know when they became afflicted. Furthermore, with many chronic diseases, it is difficult or impossible to determine the date of onset of the disease. Because a preponderance of health services and facilities are used for the treatment of persons with chronic diseases and conditions, prevalence rates are more useful than incidence rates for the planning of public health programs, personnel needs, and facilities.

An **attack rate** is a special incidence rate calculated for a particular population for a single disease outbreak and expressed as a percentage. For example, suppose a number of people who traveled on the same airline flight developed a similar illness, and epidemiologists suspected that the cause of this illness was associated with the flight itself. An attack rate could be calculated for the passengers on that flight to express the percentage who became ill. Furthermore, attack rates could be calculated for various subpopulations, such as those seated at various locations in the plane, those who selected specific entrees from the menu, those of particular age groups, or those who boarded the flight at specific stops. Differences in attack rates for different subpopulations might indicate to the epidemiologists the source or cause of the illness

Rate

In epidemiology, a rate is a measure of how frequently an event occurs, in a defined population, over a specified period of time. All rates are ratios, which simply means that they consist of one number divided by another number. The top number is called the numerator and the bottom one is the denominator. The numerator of a rate is the number of times the event of interest, such as a dog bite, occurs over a given time period. The denominator is usually the average population size (such as the population of dogs) over the same time period.

$$\text{Rate} = \frac{\text{Number of events in a specified time period}}{\text{Average population during the time period}}$$

Incidence and prevalence

They are two types of rate calculation named incidence and prevalence. These terms are used to refer to rates that measure the frequency of a disease or health condition in a population. The aim of this section is to explain what each term means, and how they differ. Prevalence refers to all (*prevAlence*) people in a defined population with the disease or condition at a given point in time or over a given period of time. The general formula for calculating the prevalence rate is as follows-

$$\text{Prevalence rate} = \frac{\text{Total number of cases in a specified time period}}{\text{Total number in the defined population}}$$

Point prevalence refers to the proportion of people in a population with a disease or condition at one point in time. **Period prevalence** is the proportion of people in a population known to have or have had a disease or condition at any time during a specified time period

Incidence differs from the prevalence in that it refers only to new (*iNcidence*) cases of a disease or condition that develop in a population over a specified period of time. The general formula for the incidence rate is as follows-

$$\text{Incidence} = \frac{\text{Number of new cases in specified time period}}{\text{Population at risk in this time period}}$$

Relationship between incidence and prevalence

The relationship between incidence and prevalence is summarized in the 'prevalence pot' (Figure 3.1). The amount of water in the bucket represents how much of a particular disease there is in the population at any one time (the point prevalence). This is dependent on the rate of new cases of the disease entering the pot (the incidence) and the rate with which people with the disease leave the pot (recover, die, or leave the area) which is related to the duration of the disease. Notice that the prevalence pot in Figure 3.1 assumes that there is no migration of people with the disease into or out of the population.

A simple mathematical formula is often used to represent the relationship between incidence, prevalence and duration of disease.

Prevalence = Incidence × Average duration of the disease

This formula is only valid in the 'steady state' (when incidence and average duration can be assumed to have been constant over a long period of time) in a population without migration, and when the prevalence of the disease is low (in other words, 10 percent or less). Nonetheless, it is a useful summary of the relationships between incidence, prevalence and duration.

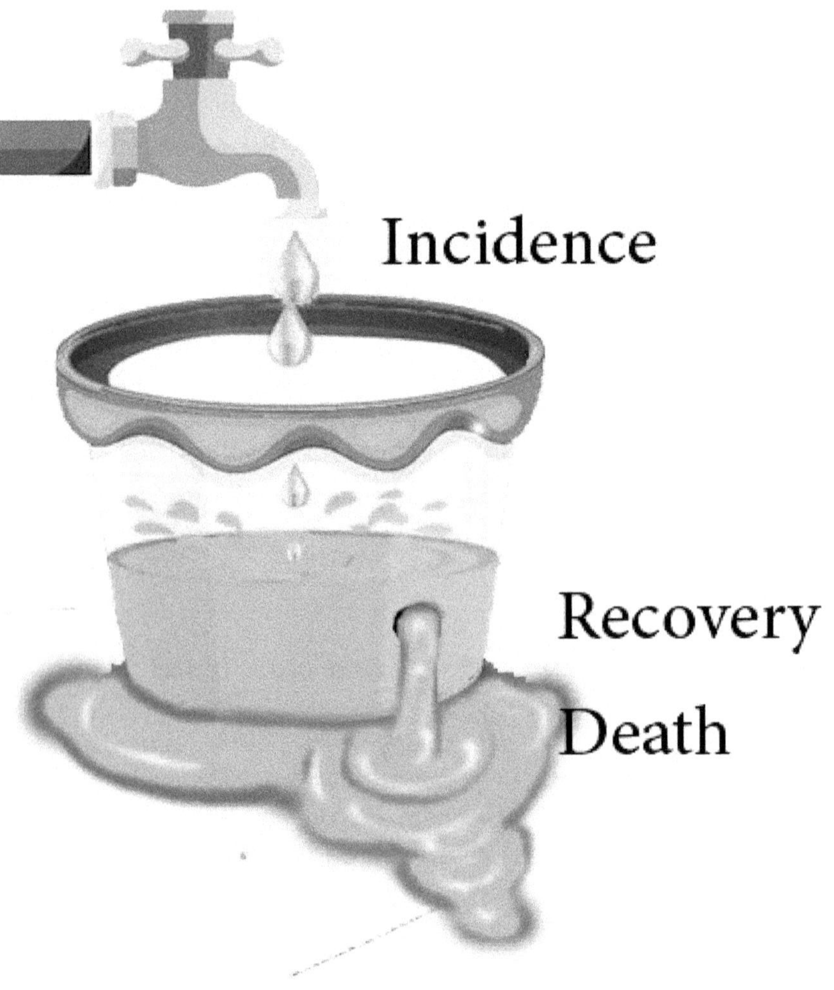

Fig 3.1 Prevalence pot

Crude, specific and standardized rates

Rates can be presented as crude, specific or standardized. A crude rate is presented for an entire population. A specific rate is presented for a particular sub-group of a population. For example, age-specific rates are those presented for specified age groups in a population; and sex-specific for men and women separately. Standardized rates are used to compare two or more populations with the effects of differences in age or other confounding variables removed. For example, one would expect a population of predominantly young adults to have a much lower crude death rate than a population of predominantly old adults. Techniques of standardization can be used to compare these two populations with the effects of the age differences removed. The uses of crude, specific and standardized rates are illustrated in the following sections on mortality rates.

Mortality rates

Mortality rate, or death rate, is a measure of the number of deaths (in general, or due to a specific cause) in a particular population, scaled to the size of that population, per unit of time. The mortality rate is typically expressed in units of deaths per 1,000 individuals per year; thus, a mortality rate of 9.5 (out of 1,000) in a population of 1,000 would mean 9.5 deaths per year in that entire population or 0.95% out of the total. It is distinct from "morbidity", which is either the prevalence or incidence of a disease and also from the incidence rate (the number of newly appearing cases of the disease per unit of time).

It was noted that routine information sources on morbidity are very limited, but that information on mortality tends to be much more readily available. For this reason, mortality rates are probably the single most important routinely available data source on the 'health' of populations. Familiarity with the use and interpretation of mortality rates is therefore very important. Mortality rates are incidence rates – the incidence of death. In the rest of this section the uses and limitations of crude, specific, and standardized mortality rates are illustrated by comparing the mortality experience of two real populations in 2001. One population is that of England and Wales, and the other is from a demographic surveillance system in Tanzania. In this system three contrasting areas of Tanzania are under surveillance, covering over 300,000 people, which is roughly 1% of the total Tanzanian population. Regular censuses are used to count the number of residents by age and sex, and a system of key informants identifies deaths.

Crude mortality rates

The crude mortality rate for a given year can be defined as:

$$\text{Mortality Rate}_{\text{Crude}} = \frac{\text{Total deaths during a the year}}{\text{Population at risk during the year}}$$

Typically mortality statistics which are routinely available, are presented for a calendar year (maybe January to December or April to March), and usually, the rate is multiplied by 1000 to give the number of deaths per 1000 population per year.

IX

Concepts of Mortality in Public health

Overview

The mortality rate is measured in per thousand. It is determined by how many people of a certain age die per thousand people. The decrease in the mortality rate is one of the reasons for the increase in population. The development of medical science and other technologies has resulted in a decrease in mortality rate in all the countries of the world for some decades. In 1990, the mortality rate of children under 5 years of age was more than 140 per thousand, but in 2015 the child mortality rate was just under 38 per thousand.

Perinatal mortality

Perinatal mortality (PNM) refers to the death of a fetus or neonate and is the basis to calculate the perinatal mortality rate. Variations in the precise definition of perinatal mortality exist, specifically concerning the issue of inclusion or exclusion of early fetal and late neonatal fatalities. The World Health Organization defines perinatal mortality as the "number of stillbirths and deaths in the first week of life per 1,000 total births, the perinatal period commences at 22 completed weeks (154 days) of gestation, and ends seven completed days after birth", but other definitions have been used.

The UK figure is about 8 per 1,000 and varies markedly by social class with the highest rates seen in Asian women. Globally, an estimated 2.6 million neonates died in 2013 before the first month of age down from 4.5 million in 1990.

Causes

Preterm birth is the most common cause of perinatal mortality, causing almost 30 percent of neonatal deaths. Infant respiratory distress syndrome, in turn, is the leading cause of death in preterm infants, affecting about 1% of newborn infants. Birth defects cause about 21 percent of neonatal death.

Fetal mortality

Fetal mortality refers to stillbirths or fetal death. It encompasses any death of a fetus after 20 weeks of gestation or 500 gm. In some definitions of the PNM early fetal mortality (week 20–27 gestation) is not included, and the PNM may only include late fetal death and neonatal death. Fetal death can also be divided into death prior to labor, antenatal (antepartum) death, and death during labor, intranatal (intrapartum) death.

Neonatal mortality

Neonatal mortality refers to death of a live-born baby within the first 28 days of life. Early neonatal mortality refers to the death of a live-born baby within the first seven days of life, while late neonatal mortality refers to death after 7 days until before 28 days. Some definitions of the PNM include only the early neonatal mortality. Neonatal mortality is affected by the quality of in-hospital care for the neonate. Neonatal mortality and postneonatal mortality (covering the remaining 11 months of the first year of life) are reflected in the infant mortality rate.

Perinatal mortality rate

The PNMR refers to the number of perinatal deaths per 1,000 total births. It is usually reported on an annual basis. It is a major marker to assess the quality of health care delivery. Comparisons between different rates may be hampered by varying definitions, registration bias, and differences in the underlying risks of the populations. PNMRs vary widely and may be below 10 for certain developed countries and more than 10 times higher in developing countries. The WHO has not published contemporary data.

Effects of neonatal nutrition on neonatal mortality

Probiotic supplementation of preterm and low birth weight babies during their first month of life can reduce the risk of blood infections, bowel sickness and death in low- and middle-income settings. However, supplementing with Vitamin A does not reduce the risk of death and increases the risk of bulging fontanelle, which may cause brain damage.

Maternal mortality

Maternal mortality is defined in slightly different ways by several different health organizations. The World Health Organization (WHO) defines maternal death as the death of a pregnant woman due to complications related to pregnancy, underlying conditions worsened by the pregnancy or management of these conditions. This can occur either while she is pregnant or within six weeks of resolution of the pregnancy. The CDC definition of pregnancy-related deaths extends the period of consideration to include one year from the resolution of the pregnancy. Pregnancy associated death, as defined by the American College of Obstetricians and Gynecologists (ACOG), are all deaths occurring within one year of a pregnancy resolution. Identification of pregnancy associated deaths is important for deciding whether or not the pregnancy was a direct or indirect contributing cause of the death.

There are two main measures used when talking about the rates of maternal mortality in a community or country. These are the maternal mortality ratio and maternal mortality rate, both abbreviated as "MMR". By 2017, the world maternal mortality rate had declined 44% since 1990; however, every day 808 women die from pregnancy or child birth related causes. According to the United Nations Population Fund (UNFPA) 2017 report, about every 2 minutes a woman dies because of complications due to child birth or pregnancy. For every woman who dies, there are about 20 to 30 women who experience injury, infection, or other birth or pregnancy related complication.

UNFPA estimated that more than three lakh women died of pregnancy or child birth related causes in 2015. The WHO divides causes of maternal deaths into two categories: direct obstetric deaths and indirect obstetric deaths. Direct obstetric deaths are causes of death due to complications of pregnancy, birth or termination. For example, these could range from severe bleeding to obstructed labor, for which there are highly effective interventions. Indirect obstetric deaths are caused by pregnancy interfering or worsening an existing condition, like a heart problem.

As women have gained access to family planning and skilled birth attendant with backup emergency obstetric care, the global maternal mortality ratio has fallen from 385 maternal deaths per 100,000 live births in 1990 to 216 deaths per 100,000 live births in 2015. Many countries halved their maternal death rates in the last 10 years. Although attempts have been made to reduce maternal mortality, there is much room for improvement, particularly in low-resource regions. Over 85% of maternal deaths are in low-resource communities in Africa and Asia. In higher resource regions, there are still significant areas with room for growth, particularly as they relate to racial and ethnic disparities and inequities in maternal mortality and morbidity rates. Overall, maternal mortality is an important marker of the overall health of the country and reflects on its health infrastructure. Lowering the amount of maternal death is an important goal of many health organizations world-wide.

Direct obstetric deaths

Direct obstetric deaths are due to complications of pregnancy, birth, termination or complications arising from their management. The causes of maternal death vary by region and level of access. According to a study published in the Lancet which covered the period from 1990 to 2013, the most common causes of maternal death world-wide are postpartum bleeding (15%), complications from unsafe abortion (15%), hypertensive disorders of pregnancy (10%), postpartum infections (8%), and obstructed labor (6%). Other causes include blood clots (3%) and pre-existing conditions (28%).

Descriptions by condition

Postpartum bleeding happens when there is uncontrollable bleeding from the uterus, cervix or vaginal wall after bleeding. This can happen when the uterus does not contract correctly after birth, there is left over placenta in the uterus, or there are cuts in the cervix or vagina from birth. Hypertensive disorders of pregnancy happen when the body does not regulate blood pressure correctly. In pregnancy, this is due to changes at the level of the blood vessels, likely because of the placenta. This includes medical conditions like gestational hypertension and pre-eclampsia. Postpartum infections are infections of the uterus or other parts of the reproductive tract after the resolution of a pregnancy. They are usually bacterial and cause fever, increased pain, and foul-smelling discharge. Obstructed labor happens when the baby does not properly move into the pelvis and out of the body during labor. The most common cause of obstructed labor is when the baby's head is too big or angled at a way that does not allow it to pass through the pelvis and birth canal. Blood clots can occur in different vessels in the body, including vessels in the arms, legs, and lungs. They can cause problems in the lung, as well as travel to the heart or brain, leading to complications.

Abortion

When abortion is legal and accessible, it is widely regarded as safer than carrying a pregnancy to term and delivery. In fact, a study published in the journal Obstetrics & Gynecology reported that in the United States, carrying a pregnancy to term and delivering a baby comes with 14 times increased risk of death as compared to a legal abortion. However, in many regions of the world, abortion is not legal and can be unsafe. Maternal deaths caused by improperly performed procedures are preventable and contribute 13% to the maternal mortality rate worldwide. This number is increased to 25% in countries where other causes of maternal mortality are low, such as in Eastern European and South American countries. This makes unsafe abortion practices the leading cause of maternal death worldwide. Unsafe abortion is another major cause of maternal death worldwide. In regions where abortion is legal and accessible, abortion is safe and does not contribute greatly to overall rates of maternal death. However, in regions where abortions are not legal, available, or regulated, unsafe abortion practices can cause significant rates of maternal death. According to the World Health Organization in 2009, every eight minutes a woman died from complications arising from unsafe abortions.

Unsafe abortion practices are defined by the WHO as procedures that are performed by someone without the appropriate training and/or ones that are performed in an environment that is not considered safe or clean. Using this definition, the WHO estimates that out of the 45 million abortions that are performed each year globally, 19 million of these are considered unsafe, and 97% of these unsafe abortions occur in developing countries. Complications include hemorrhage, infection, sepsis and genital trauma.

Indirect obstetric deaths

Indirect obstetric deaths are caused by preexisting health problems worsened by pregnancy or newly developed health problems unrelated to pregnancy. Fatalities during but unrelated to a pregnancy are termed accidental, incidental, or non-obstetrical maternal deaths. Indirect causes include malaria, anemia, HIV/AIDS, and cardiovascular disease, all of which may complicate pregnancy or be aggravated by it. Risk factors associated with increased maternal death include the age of the mother, obesity before becoming pregnant, other pre-existing chronic medical conditions, and cesarean delivery.

Severe maternal morbidity

Severe maternal morbidity (SMM) is an unanticipated acute or chronic health outcome after labor and delivery that detrimentally affects a woman's health. Severe Maternal Morbidity (SMM) includes any unexpected outcomes from labor or delivery that cause both short and long-term consequences to the mother's overall health. There are nineteen total indicators used by the CDC to help identify SMM, with the most prevalent indicator being a blood transfusion. Other indicators include an acute myocardial infarction ("heart attack"), aneurysm, and kidney failure. All of this identification is done by using ICD-10 codes, which are disease identification codes found in hospital discharge data. Using these definitions that rely on these codes should be used with careful consideration since some may miss some cases, have a low predictive value, or may be difficult for different facilities to operationalize. There are certain screening criteria that may be helpful and are recommended through the American College of Obstetricians and Gynecologists as well as the Society for Maternal-Fetal Medicine (SMFM). These screening criteria for SMM are for transfusions of four or more units of blood and admission of a pregnant woman or a postpartum woman to an ICU facility or unit. The greatest proportion of women with SMM are those who require a blood transfusion during delivery, mostly due to excessive bleeding. Blood transfusions given during delivery due to excessive bleeding has increased the rate of mothers with SMM. The rate of SMM has increased almost 200% between 1993 (49.5 per 100,000 live births) and 2014 (144.0 per 100,000 live births). This can be seen with the increased rate of blood transfusions given during delivery, which increased from 1993 (24.5 per 100,000 live births) to 2014 (122.3 per 100,000 live births).

In the United States, severe maternal morbidity has increased over the last several years, impacting greater than 50,000 women in 2014 alone. There is no conclusive reason for this dramatic increase. It is thought that the overall state of health for pregnant women is impacting these rates. For example, complications can derive from underlying chronic medical conditions like diabetes, obesity, HIV/AIDS, and high blood pressure. These underlying conditions are also thought to lead to increased risk of maternal mortality.The increased rate for SMM can also be indicative of potentially increased rates for maternal mortality, since without identification and treatment of SMM, these conditions would lead to increased maternal death rates. Therefore, diagnosis of SMM can be considered a "near miss" for maternal mortality. With this consideration, several different expert groups have urged obstetric hospitals to review SMM cases for opportunities that can lead to improved care, which in turn would lead to improvements with maternal health and a decrease in the number of maternal deaths.

Overall risk factors of maternal death

In, 2004 WHO delivered its concern through a published article on sociodemographic factors such as age, access to resources and income level are significant indicators of maternal outcomes. Young mothers face higher risks of complications and death during pregnancy than older mothers, especially adolescents aged 15 years or younger. Adolescents have higher risks or postpartum hemorrhage, endometritis, operative vaginal delivery, episiotomy, low birth weight, preterm delivery, and small-for-gestational-age infants, all of which can lead to maternal death. The leading cause of death for girls at the age of 15 in developing complications through pregnancy and childbirth. They have more pregnancies, on average, than women in developed countries, and it has been shown that 1 in 180 15-year-old girls in developing countries who become pregnant will die due to complications during pregnancy or childbirth. This is compared to women in developed countries, where the likelihood is 1 in 4900 live births. However, in the United States, as many women of older age continue to have children, the maternal mortality rate has risen in some states, especially among women over 40 years old.

Structural support and family support influence maternal outcomes. Furthermore, social disadvantage and social isolation adversely affect maternal health which can lead to increases in maternal death. Additionally, lack of access to skilled medical care during childbirth, the travel distance to the nearest clinic to receive proper care, number of prior births, barriers to accessing prenatal medical care and poor infrastructure all increase maternal deaths.

Three delays model

The three delays model addresses three critical factors that inhibit women from receiving appropriate maternal health care. The factors are as follows:

- Delay in seeking care
- Delay in reaching care
- Delay in receiving adequate and appropriate care

Delays in seeking care are due to the decisions made by the women who are pregnant and/or other decision-making individuals. Decision-making individuals can include a spouse and family members. Examples of reasons for delays in seeking care include lack of knowledge about when to seek care, inability to afford health care, and women needing permission from family members. Delays in reaching care include factors such as limitations in transportation to a medical facility, lack of adequate medical facilities in the area, and lack in confidence in medicine. Delays in receiving adequate and appropriate care may result from an inadequate number of trained providers, lack of appropriate supplies, and the lack of urgency or understanding of an emergency. The three delays model illustrates that there are a multitude of complex factors, both socioeconomic and cultural, that can result in maternal death.

Trends of maternal mortality

The United Nations Population Fund (UNFPA; formerly known as the United Nations Fund for Population Activities) has established programs that support efforts in reducing maternal death. These efforts include education and training for midwives, supporting access to emergency services in obstetric and newborn care networks, and providing essential drugs and family planning services to pregnant women or those planning to become pregnant. They also support efforts for review and response systems regarding maternal deaths. According to the 2010 United Nations Population Fund report, low-resource nations account for ninety-nine percent of maternal deaths with the majority of those deaths occurring in Sub-Saharan Africa and Southern Asia. Globally, high and middle income countries experience lower maternal deaths than low income countries. The Human Development Index (HDI) accounts for between 82 - 85% of the maternal mortality rates among countries. In most cases, high rates of maternal deaths occur in the same countries that have high rates of infant mortality. These trends are a reflection that higher income countries have stronger healthcare infrastructure, more doctors, use more advanced medical technologies and have fewer barriers to accessing care than low income countries. In low income countries, the most common cause of maternal death is obstetrical hemorrhage, followed by hypertensive disorders of pregnancy. This is contrast to high income countries, for which the most common cause is thromboembolism.

Between 1990 to 2015, the maternal mortality ratio decreased from 385 deaths per 100,000 live births to 216 maternal deaths per 100,000 live births. Some factors that have been attributed to the decreased maternal deaths seen during this period are in part to the access that women have gained to family planning services and skilled birth attendance, meaning a midwife, doctor, or trained nurse), with backup obstetric care for emergency situations that may occur during the process of labor. This can be examined further by looking at statistics in some areas of the world where inequities in access to health care services reflect an increased number of maternal deaths. The high maternal death rates also reflect disparate access to health services between resource communities and those that are high-resource or affluent. The disparities in maternal health outcomes are also present among racial groups. In USA, Afro-American women are 3-4 times more likely to die from maternal mortality than white women. Unequal access to quality medical care, socioeconomic disparities, and systemic racism by health care providers are factors that have contributed to the high maternal mortality rates among Afro-American women.

Measurement of maternal mortality

The four measures of maternal death are the maternal mortality ratio (MMR), maternal mortality rate, lifetime risk of maternal death and proportion of maternal deaths among deaths of women of reproductive years (PM). Maternal mortality ratio (MMR) is the ratio of the number of maternal deaths during a given time period per 100,000 live births during the same time period. The MMR is used as a measure of the quality of a health care system. Maternal mortality rate (MMRate) is the number of maternal deaths in a population divided by the number of women of reproductive age, usually expressed per 1,000 women.

Lifetime risk of maternal death is a calculated prediction of a woman's risk of death after each consecutive pregnancy. The calculation pertains to women during their reproductive years. The adult lifetime risk of maternal mortality can be derived using either the maternal mortality ratio (MMR), or the maternal mortality rate (MMRate). Proportion of maternal deaths among deaths of women of reproductive age (PM) is the number of maternal deaths in a given time period divided by the total deaths among women aged 15–49 years. Approaches to measuring maternal mortality include civil registration system, household surveys, census, reproductive age mortality studies (RAMOS) and verbal autopsies. The most common household survey method, recommended by the WHO as time- and cost-effective, is the sisterhood method.

Prevention

According to UNFPA, there are four essential elements for prevention of maternal death. These include, prenatal care, assistance with birth, access to emergency obstetric care and adequate postnatal care. It is recommended that expectant mothers receive at least four antenatal visits to check and monitor the health of mother and fetus. Second, skilled birth attendance with emergency backup such as doctors, nurses and midwives who have the skills to manage normal deliveries and recognize the onset of complications.

Third, emergency obstetric care to address the major causes of maternal death which are hemorrhage, sepsis, unsafe abortion, hypertensive disorders and obstructed labor. Lastly, postnatal care which is the six weeks following delivery. During this time, bleeding, sepsis and hypertensive disorders can occur, and newborns are extremely vulnerable in the immediate aftermath of birth. Therefore, follow-up visits by a health worker to assess the health of both mother and child in the postnatal period is strongly recommended. Additionally, reliable access to information, compassionate counseling and quality services for the management of any issues that arise from abortions (whether safe or unsafe) can be beneficial in reducing the number of maternal deaths. In regions where abortion is legal, abortion practices need to be safe in order to effectively reduce the number of maternal deaths related to abortion.

Maternal Death Surveillance and Response is another strategy that has been used to prevent maternal death. This is one of the interventions proposed to reduce maternal mortality where maternal deaths are continuously reviewed to learn the causes and factors that led to the death. The information from the reviews is used to make recommendations for action to prevent future similar deaths. Maternal and perinatal death reviews have been in practice for a long time worldwide, and the World Health Organization (WHO) introduced the Maternal and Perinatal Death Surveillance and Response (MPDSR) with a guideline in 2013. Studies have shown that acting on recommendations from MPDSR can reduce maternal and perinatal mortality by improving quality of care in the community and health facilities.

Prenatal care

It was estimated that in 2015, a total of 303,000 women died due to causes related to pregnancy or childbirth. The majority of these were due to severe bleeding, sepsis or infections, eclampsia, obstructed labor, and consequences from unsafe abortions. Most of these causes are either preventable or have highly effective interventions. An important factor that contributes to the maternal mortality rate is access and the opportunity to receive prenatal care. Women who do not receive prenatal care are between three and four times more likely to die from complications resulting from pregnancy or delivery than those who receive prenatal care. Even in high-resource countries, many women do not receive the appropriate preventative or prenatal care. For example, 25% of women in the United States do not receive the recommended number of prenatal visits. This number increases for women among traditionally marginalized populations—32% of African American women and 41% of American Indian and Alaska Native women do not receive the recommended preventative health services prior to delivery.

Medical technologies

The decline in maternal deaths has been due largely to improved aseptic techniques, better fluid management and quicker access to blood transfusions, and better prenatal care. Technologies have been designed for resource-poor settings that have been effective in reducing maternal deaths as well. The non-pneumatic anti-shock garment is a low-technology pressure device that decreases blood loss, restores vital signs and helps buy time in the delay of women receiving adequate emergency care during obstetric hemorrhage. It has proven to be a valuable resource. Condoms used as uterine tamponades have also been effective in stopping post-partum hemorrhage.

Medications and surgical management

Some maternal deaths can be prevented through medication use. Injectable oxytocin can be used to prevent death due to postpartum bleeding. Additionally, postpartum infections can be treated using antibiotics. In fact, the use of broad-spectrum antibiotics both for the prevention and treatment of maternal infection is common in low-income countries. Maternal death due to eclampsia can also be prevented through the use of medications such as magnesium sulfate. Many complications can be managed with procedures and/or surgery if there is access to a qualified surgeon and appropriate facilities and supplies. For example, the contents of the uterus can be cleaned if there is concern for remaining pregnancy tissue or infection. If there is concern for excess bleeding, special ties, stitches or tools (Bakri Balloon) can be placed if there is concern for excess bleeding.

Public health approach

A public health approach to addressing maternal mortality includes gathering information on the scope of the problem, identifying key causes, and implementing interventions, both prior to pregnancy and during pregnancy, to combat those causes and prevent maternal mortality. Public health has a role to play in the analysis of maternal death. One important aspect in the review of maternal death and its causes are Maternal Mortality Review Committees or Boards. The goal of these review committees are to analyze each maternal death and determine its cause. After this analysis, the information can be combined in order to determine specific interventions that could lead to preventing future maternal deaths. These review boards are generally comprehensive in their analysis of maternal deaths, examining details that include mental health factors, public transportation, chronic illnesses, and substance use disorders. All of this information can be combined to give a detailed picture of what is causing maternal mortality and help to determine recommendations to reduce their impact. Many states within the US are taking Maternal Mortality Review Committees a step further and are collaborating with various professional organizations to improve quality of perinatal care. These teams of organizations form a "perinatal quality collaborative" (PQC) and include state health departments, the state hospital association and clinical professionals such as doctors and nurses. These PQCs can also involve community health organizations, Medicaid representatives, Maternal Mortality Review Committees and patient advocacy groups. By involving all of these major players within maternal health, the goal is to collaborate and determine opportunities to improve quality of care. Through this collaborative effort, PQCs can aim to make impacts on quality both at the direct patient care level and through larger system devices like policy. It is thought that the institution of PQCs in California was the main contributor to the maternal mortality rate decreasing by 50% in the years following. The PQC developed review guides and quality improvement initiatives aimed at the most preventable and prevalent maternal deaths: those due to bleeding and high blood pressure. Success has also been observed with PQCs in Illinois and Florida.

Several interventions prior to pregnancy have been recommended in efforts to reduce maternal mortality. Increasing access to reproductive healthcare services, such as family planning services and safe abortion practices, is recommended in order to prevent unintended pregnancies. Several countries, including India, Brazil, and Mexico, have seen some success in efforts to promote the use of reproductive healthcare services.

Other interventions include high quality sex education, which includes pregnancy prevention and sexually transmitted infection (STI) prevention and treatment. Addressing STIs, not only reduces perinatal infections, but can also help reduce ectopic pregnancy caused by STIs. Adolescents are between two and five times more likely to suffer from maternal mortality than a female twenty years or older. Access to reproductive services and sex education could make a large impact, specifically on adolescents, who are generally uneducated in regards to carrying a healthy pregnancy. Education level is a strong predictor of maternal health as it gives women the knowledge to seek care when it is needed. Public health efforts can also intervene during pregnancy to improve maternal outcomes. Areas for intervention have been identified in access to care, public knowledge, awareness about signs and symptoms of pregnancy complications, and improving relationships between healthcare professionals and expecting mothers. Access to care during pregnancy is a significant issue in the face of maternal mortality. "Access" encompasses a wide range of potential difficulties including costs, location of healthcare services, availability of appointments, availability of trained health care workers, transportation services, and cultural or language barriers that could inhibit a woman from receiving proper care. For women carrying a pregnancy to term, access to necessary antenatal (prior to delivery) healthcare visits is crucial to ensuring healthy outcomes. These antenatal visits allow for early recognition and treatment of complications, treatment of infections and the opportunity to educate the expecting mother on how to manage her current pregnancy and the health advantages of spacing pregnancies apart.

Access to birth at a facility with a skilled healthcare provider present has been associated with safer deliveries and better outcomes. The two areas bearing the largest burden of maternal mortality, Sub-Saharan Africa and South Asia, also had the lowest percentage of births attended by a skilled provider, at just 45% and 41% respectively. Emergency obstetric care is also crucial in preventing maternal mortality by offering services like emergency cesarean sections, blood transfusions, antibiotics for infections and assisted vaginal delivery with forceps or vacuum. In addition to physical barriers that restrict access to healthcare, financial barriers also exist. Close to one out of seven women of child-bearing age have no health insurance. This lack of insurance impacts access to pregnancy prevention, treatment of complications, as well as perinatal care visits contributing to maternal mortality. By increasing public knowledge and awareness through health education programs about pregnancy, including signs of complications that need addressed by a healthcare provider, this will increase the likelihood of an expecting mother seeking help when it is necessary. Higher levels of education have been associated with increased use of contraception and family planning services as well as antenatal care. Addressing complications at the earliest sign of a problem can improve outcomes for expecting mothers, which makes it extremely important for a pregnant woman to be knowledgeable enough to seek healthcare for potential complications. Improving the relationships between patients and the healthcare system as a whole will make it easier for a pregnant woman to feel comfortable seeking help. Good communication between patients and providers, as well as cultural competence of the providers, could also assist in increasing compliance with recommended treatments. Another important preventive measure being implemented is specialized education for mothers. Doctors and medical professionals providing simple information to women, especially women in lower socioeconomic areas will decrease the miscommunication that often occurs between doctors and patients. Training health care professionals will be another important aspect in decreasing the rate of maternal death, "The study found that white medical students and residents often believed incorrect and sometimes 'fantastical' biological fallacies about racial differences in patients. For these assumptions, researchers blamed not individual prejudice but deeply ingrained unconscious stereotypes about people of color, as well as physicians' difficulty in empathizing with patients whose experiences differ from their own."

Policy

The biggest global policy initiative for maternal health came from the United Nations' Millennium Declaration which created the Millennium Development Goals. In 2012, this evolved at the United Nations Conference on Sustainable Development to become the Sustainable Development Goals (SDGs) with a target year of 2030. The SDGs are 17 goals that call for global collaboration to tackle a wide variety of recognized problems. Goal 3 is focused on ensuring health and well-being for people of all ages. A specific target is to achieve a global maternal mortality ratio of less than 70 per 100,000 live births. So far, specific progress has been made in births attended by a skilled provider, now at 80% of births worldwide compared with 62% in 2005. Countries and local governments have taken political steps in reducing maternal deaths. Researchers at the Overseas Development Institute studied maternal health systems in four apparently similar countries: Rwanda, Malawi, Niger, and Uganda. In comparison to the other three countries, Rwanda has an excellent recent record of improving maternal death rates. Based on their investigation of these varying country case studies, the researchers conclude that improving maternal health depends on three key factors as follows:

1. Reviewing all maternal health-related policies frequently to ensure that they are internally coherent.
2. Enforcing standards on providers of maternal health services.
3. Any local solutions to problems discovered should be promoted, not discouraged.

In terms of aid policy, proportionally, aid given to improve maternal mortality rates has shrunken as other public health issues, such as HIV/AIDS and malaria have become major international concerns. Maternal health aid contributions tend to be lumped together with newborn and child health, so it is difficult to assess how much aid is given directly to maternal health to help lower the rates of maternal mortality. Regardless, there has been progressing in reducing maternal mortality rates internationally. In countries where abortion practices are not considered legal, it is necessary to look at the access that women have to high-quality family planning services since some of the restrictive policies around abortion could impede access to these services. These policies may also affect the proper collection of information for monitoring maternal health around the world.

Epidemology

Maternal deaths and disabilities are leading contributors in women's disease burden with an estimated 303,000 women killed each year in childbirth and pregnancy worldwide.\ The global rate in 2017 is 211 maternal deaths per 100,000 live births and 45% of postpartum deaths occur within 24 hours. Ninety-nine percent of maternal deaths occur in low-resource countries.

At a country level, India (19% or 56,000) and Nigeria (14% or 40,000) scounted for roughly one third of the maternal deaths in 2010. Democratic

Republic of the Congo, Pakistan, Sudan, Indonesia, Ethiopia, United Republic of Tanzania, Bangladesh and Afghanistan accounted for between 3 and 5 percent of maternal deaths each. These ten countries combined accounted for 60% of all the maternal deaths in 2010 according to the United Nations Population Fund report. Countries with the lowest maternal deaths were Greece, Iceland, Poland, and Finland.

As of 2017, countries in Southeast Asia and Sub-Saharan Africa account for approximately 86% of all maternal death in the world. Sub-Saharan African countries accounted for about two-thirds of the global maternal deaths and Southeast Asian countries accounted for approximately one-fifth. Since 2000, Southeast Asian countries have seen a significant decrease in maternal mortality with an overall decrease in maternal mortality of almost 60%. Sub-Saharan Africa also saw an almost 40% decrease in maternal mortality between 2000 and 2017. As of 2017, the countries with the highest maternal mortality rates included South Sudan, Somalia, Central African Republic, Yemen, Syria, South Sudan, and the Democratic Republic of the Congo. The numbers for maternal mortality in these countries are likely affect by the political and civil unrest that these countries are facing. Significant progress has been made since the United Nations made the reduction of maternal mortality part of the Millennium Development Goals (MDGs) in 2000.

Bangladesh, for example, cut the number of deaths per live births by almost two-thirds from 1990 to 2015. A further reduction of maternal mortality is now part of the Agenda 2030 for sustainable development. The United Nations has more recently developed a list of goals termed the Sustainable Development Goals. The target of the third Sustainable Development Goal (SDG) is to reduce the global maternal mortality rate (MMR) to less than 70 per 100,000 live births by 2030. Some of the specific aims of the Sustainable Development Goals are to prevent unintended pregnancies by ensuring more women have access to contraceptives, as well as providing women who become pregnant with a safe environment for delivery with respectful and skilled care. This initiative also included access to emergency services for women who developed complications during delivery. The WHO has developed a global goal to end preventable death related to maternal mortality. A major goal of this strategy is to identify and address the causes of maternal and reproductive morbidities and mortalities, as well as disabilities related to maternal health outcomes. Their strategy aims to address inequalities in access to reproductive, maternal, and newborn services, as well as the quality of care with universal health coverage. The WHO strategy also aims to ensure quality data collection in order to better respond to the needs of women and girls while improving the equity and quality of care provided to women.

Variation within countries

There are significant maternal mortality intra country variations, especially in nations with large equality gaps in income and education and high healthcare disparities. Women living in rural areas experience higher maternal mortality than women living in urban and sub-urban centers because those living in wealthier households, having higher education, or living in urban areas, have higher use of healthcare services than their poorer, less-educated, or rural counterparts. There are also racial and ethnic disparities in maternal health outcomes which increases maternal mortality in marginalized groups.

Maternal deaths and disabilities are leading contributors in women's disease burden with an estimated 303,000 women killed each year in childbirth and pregnancy worldwide. The global rate in 2017 is 211 maternal deaths per 100,000 live births and 45% of postpartum deaths occur within 24 hours. Ninety-nine percent of maternal deaths occur in low-resource countries. At a country level, India (19% or 56,000) and Nigeria (14% or 40,000) accounted for roughly one third of the maternal deaths in 2010. Democratic Republic of the Congo, Pakistan, Sudan, Indonesia, Ethiopia, United Republic of Tanzania, Bangladesh and Afghanistan accounted for between 3 and 5 percent of maternal deaths each. These ten countries combined accounted for 60% of all the maternal deaths in 2010 according to the United Nations Population Fund report. Countries with the lowest maternal deaths were Greece, Iceland, Poland, and Finland.

As of 2017, countries in Southeast Asia and Sub-Saharan Africa account for approximately 86% of all maternal death in the world. Sub-Saharan African countries accounted for about two-thirds of the global maternal deaths and Southeast Asian countries accounted for approximately one-fifth. Since 2000, Southeast Asian countries have seen a significant decrease in maternal mortality with an overall decrease in maternal mortality of almost 60%. Sub-Saharan Africa also saw an almost 40% decrease in maternal mortality between 2000 and 2017. As of 2017, the countries with the highest maternal mortality rates included South Sudan, Somalia,

Central African Republic, Yemen, Syria, South Sudan, and the Democratic Republic of the Congo. The numbers for maternal mortality in these countries are likely affected by the political and civil unrest that these countries are facing.

Significant progress has been made since the United Nations made the reduction of maternal mortality part of the Millennium Development Goals (MDGs) in 2000.:1066 Bangladesh, for example, cut the number of deaths per live birth by almost two-thirds from 1990 to 2015. A further reduction of maternal mortality is now part of the Agenda 2030 for sustainable development. The United Nations has more recently developed a list of goals termed the Sustainable Development Goals. The target of the third Sustainable Development Goal (SDG) is to reduce the global maternal mortality rate (MMR) to less than 70 per 100,000 live births by 2030. Some of the specific aims of the Sustainable Development Goals are to prevent unintended pregnancies by ensuring more women have access to contraceptives, as well as providing women who become pregnant with a safe environment for delivery with respectful and skilled care. This initiative also included access to emergency services for women who developed complications during delivery. The WHO has developed a global goal to end preventable death related to maternal mortality. A major goal of this strategy is to identify and address the causes of maternal and reproductive morbidities and mortalities, as well as disabilities related to maternal health outcomes. Their strategy aims to address inequalities in access to reproductive, maternal, and newborn services, as well as the quality of care with universal health coverage. The WHO strategy also aims to ensure quality data collection in order to better respond to the needs of women and girls while improving the equity and quality of care provided to women.

X

Survey: Methods and Outcome

Introduction

Survey methodology is "the study of survey methods". As a field of applied statistics concentrating on human-research surveys, survey methodology studies the sampling of individual units from a population and associated techniques of survey data collection, such as questionnaire construction and methods for improving the number and accuracy of responses to surveys. Survey methodology targets instruments or procedures that ask one or more questions that may or may not be answered. Researchers carry out statistical surveys with a view towards making statistical inferences about the population being studied; such inferences depend strongly on the survey questions used. Polls about public opinion, public-health surveys, market-research surveys, government surveys and censuses all exemplify quantitative research that uses survey methodology to answer questions about a population. Although censuses do not include a "sample", they do include other aspects of survey methodology, like questionnaires, interviewers, and non-response follow-up techniques. Surveys provide important information for all kinds of public-information and research fields, such as marketing research, psychology, health-care provision and sociology.

The survey is a popular means of gauging people's opinion of a particular topic, such as their perception or reported use of a particular health system. Yet surveying as a scientific approach is often misconstrued. And while a survey seems easy to conduct, ensuring that it is of high quality is much more difficult to achieve. Often the terms "survey" and "questionnaire" are used interchangeably as if they are the same. But strictly speaking, the survey is a research approach where subjective opinions are collected from a sample of subjects and analyzed for some aspects of the study population that they represent. On the other hand, a questionnaire is one of the data collection methods used in the survey approach, where subjects are asked to respond to a predefined set of questions.

The literature is replete with survey studies conducted in different health settings on a variety of topics, for example the perceived satisfaction of ehr systems by ophthalmologists in the United States (Chiang et al., 2008), and the reported impact of emr adoption in primary care in a Canadian province (Paré et al., 2013). The quality of eHealth survey studies can be highly variable depending on how they are designed, conducted, analyzed and reported. It is important to point out there are different types of survey studies that range in nature from the exploratory to the predictive, involving one or more groups of subjects and an eHealth system over a given time period. There are also various published guidelines on how survey studies should be designed, reported and appraised. Increasingly, survey studies are used by health organizations to learn about provider, patient and public perceptions toward eHealth systems. As a consequence, the types of survey studies and their methodological considerations should be of great interest to those involved with eHealth evaluation.

This chapter describes the types of survey studies used in eHealth evaluation and their methodological considerations. Also included are three case examples to show how these studies are done.

Types of Survey Studies

There are different types of survey study designs depending on the intended purpose and approach taken. Within a given type of survey design, there are different design options with respect to the time period, respondent group, variable choice, data collection and analytical method involved. These design features are described below (Williamson & Johanson, 2013).

The Purpose of Surveys

There are three broad types of survey studies reported in the eHealth literature: exploratory, descriptive, and explanatory surveys. They are described below.

Exploratory Surveys

These studies are used to investigate and understand a particular issue or topic area without predetermined notions of the expected responses. The design is mostly qualitative in nature, seeking input from respondents with open-ended questions focused on why and/or how they perceive certain aspects of an electronic health system. For an example, the survey by Wells, Rozenblum, Park, Dunn, and Bates (2014) to identify organizational strategies that promote provider and patient uptake of phrs.

Descriptive Surveys

These studies are used to describe the perception of respondents and the association of their characteristics with an eHealth system. Perception can be the attitudes, behaviours and reported interactions of respondents with the eHealth system. Association refers to an observed correlation between certain respondent characteristics and the system, such as prior eHealth experience. The design is mostly quantitative and involves the use of descriptive statistics such as frequency distributions of Likert scale responses from participants. An example is the survey on change in end user satisfaction with CPOE over time in intensive care (Hoonakker et al., 2013).

Explanatory Surveys

These studies are used to explain or predict one or more hypothesized relationships between some respondent characteristics and the eHealth system. The design is quantitative, involving the use of inferential statistics such as regression and factor analysis to quantify the extent to which certain respondent characteristics lead to or are associated with specific outcomes. An example is the survey to model certain residential care facility characteristics as predictors of ehr use (Holup, Dobbs, Meng, & Hyer, 2013).

Survey Design Options

Within the three broad types of survey studies one can further distinguish their design by time period, respondent group, variable choice, data collection and analytical method. These survey design options are described below.

Time Period

Surveys can take on a cross-sectional or longitudinal design based on the time period involved. In cross-sectional design the survey takes place at one point in time giving a snapshot of the participant responses. In longitudinal design the survey is repeated two or more times within a specified period in order to detect changes in participant responses over time.

Respondent Group

Surveys can involve a single or multiple cohorts of respondents. With multiple cohorts they are typically grouped by some characteristics for comparison such as age, sex, or eHealth use status (e.g., users versus non-users of emr).

Variable Choice

In quantitative surveys one needs to define the dependent and independent variables being studied. A dependent variable refers to the perceived outcome that is measured, whereas an independent variable refers to a respondent characteristic that may influence the outcome (such as age). Typically the variables are defined using a scale that can be nominal, ordinal, interval, or ratio in nature (Layman & Watzlaf, 2009). In a nominal scale, a value is assigned to each response such as 1 or F for female and 2 or M for male. In an ordinal scale, the response can be rank ordered such as user satisfaction that starts from 1 for very unsatisfied to 4 for very satisfied. Interval and ratio scales have numerical meaning where the distance between two responses relate to the numerical values assigned. Ratio is different from interval in that it has a natural zero point. Two examples are weight as a ratio scale and temperature as an interval scale.

Data Collection

Surveys can be conducted by questionnaire or by interview with structured, semi-structured or non-structured questions. Questionnaires can be administered by postal mail, telephone, e-mail, or through a website. Interviews can be conducted in-person or by phone individually or in groups. Pretesting or pilot testing of the instrument should be done with a small number of individuals to ensure its content, flow and instructions are clear, consistent, appropriate and easy to follow. Usually there are one or more follow-up reminders sent to increase the response rate.

Analytical Method

Survey responses are analyzed in different ways depending on the type of data collected. For textual data such qualitative analyses as content or thematic analysis can be used. Content analysis focuses on classifying words and phrases within the texts into categories based on some initial coding scheme and frequency counts. Thematic analysis focuses on identifying concepts, relationships and patterns from texts as themes. For numeric data, quantitative analysis such as descriptive and inferential statistics can be used. Descriptive statistics involves the use of such measures as mean, range, standard deviation and frequency to summarize the distribution of numeric data. Inferential statistics involve the use of a random sample of data from the study population to make inferences about that population. The inferences are made with parametric and non-parametric tests and multivariate methods. Pearson correlation, t-test and analysis of variance are examples of parametric tests. Sign test, Mann-Witney U test and $\chi 2$ are examples of non-parametric tests. Multiple regression, multivariate analysis of variance, and factor analysis are examples of multivariate methods (Forza, 2002).

Methodological Considerations

The quality of survey studies is dependent on a number of design parameters. These include population and sample, survey instrument, sources of bias, and adherence to reporting standards. These considerations are described below (Williamson & Johanson, 2013).

Population and Sample

For practical reasons, survey studies are often done on a sample of individuals rather than the entire population. Sampling frame refers to the population of interest from which a representative sample is drawn for the study. The two common strategies used to select the study sample are probability and non-probability sampling. These are described below.

Probability sampling

This is used in descriptive and explanatory surveys where the sample selected is based on the statistical probability of each individual being included under the assumption of normal distribution. They include such methods as simple random, systematic, stratified, and cluster sampling. The desired confidence level and margin of error are used to determine the required sample size. For example, in a population of 250,000 at 95% confidence level and a ±5% margin of error, a sample of 384 individuals is needed.

Non-probability sampling – This is used in exploratory surveys where individuals with specific characteristics that can help understand the topic being investigated are selected as the sample. They include such non-statistical methods as a convenience, snowball, quota, and purposeful sampling. For example, to study the effects of the Internet on patients with chronic conditions one can employ purposeful sampling where only individuals known to have a chronic disease and access to the Internet are selected for inclusion.

Survey Instrument

The survey instrument is the tool used to collect data from respondents on the topic being investigated. Ideally one should demonstrate that the survey instrument chosen is both valid and reliable for use in the study. Validity refers to whether the items (i.e., predefined questions and responses) in the instrument are accurate in what they intend to measure. Reliability refers to the extent to which the data collected are reproducible when repeated on the same or similar groups of respondents. These two constructs are elaborated below.

Validity

The four types of validity are known as face, content, criterion, and construct validity. Face and content validity are qualitative assessments of the survey instrument for its clarity, comprehensibility and appropriateness. While face validity is typically assessed informally by non-experts, content validity is done formally by experts in the subject matter under study. Criterion and construct validity are quantitative assessments where the instrument is measured against other schemes. In criterion validity the instrument is compared with another reputable test on the same respondents, or against actual future outcomes for the survey's predictive ability. In construct validity the instrument is compared with the theoretical concepts that the instrument purports to represent to see how well the two align with each other.

Reliability

The tests for reliability include test-retest, alternate form and internal consistency. Test-retest reliability correlates results from the same survey instrument administered to the same respondents over two time periods. Alternate form reliability correlates results from different versions of the same instrument on the same or similar individuals. Internal consistency reliability measures how well different items in the same survey that measure the same construct produce similar results.

Sources of Bias

There are four potential sources of bias in survey studies. These are coverage, sampling, non-response, and measurement errors. These potential biases and ways to minimize them are described below.

Coverage bias

This occurs when the sampling frame is not representative of the study population such that certain segments of the population are excluded or under-represented. For instance, the use of the telephone directory to select participants would exclude those with unlisted numbers and mobile devices. To address this error one needs to employ multiple sources to select samples that are more representative of the population. For example, in a telephone survey of consumers on their eHealth attitudes and experience, Ancker, Silver, Miller, and Kaushal (2013) included both landline and cell phone to recruit consumers since young adults, men and minorities tend to be under-represented among those with landlines.

Sampling bias

This occurs when the sample selected for the study is not representative of the population such that the sample values cannot be generalized to the broader population. For example, in their survey of provider satisfaction and reported usage of cpoe, Lee, Teich, Spurr, and Bates (1996) reported different response rates between physicians and nurses, and between medical and surgical staffs, which could affect the generalizability of the results. To avoid sampling bias one should clearly define the target population and sampling frame, employ systematic methods such as stratified or random sampling to select samples, identify the extent and causes of response differences, and adjust the analysis and interpretation accordingly.

Non-response bias

This occurs when individuals who responded to the survey have different attributes than those who did not respond to the survey. For example, in their study to model nurses' acceptance of barcoded medication administration technology, Holden, Brown, Scanlon, and Karsh (2012) acknowledged their less than 50% response rate could have led to non-response bias affecting the accuracy of their prediction model. To address this error one can offer incentives to increase response rate, follow up with non-respondents to find out the reasons for their lack of response, or compare the characteristics of non-respondents with respondents or known external benchmarks for differences (King & He, 2005). Adjustments can then be made when the cause and extent of non-response are known.

Measurement bias

This occurs when there is a difference between the survey results obtained and the true values in the population. One major cause is deficient instrument design due to ambiguous items, unclear instructions, or poor usability. To reduce measurement bias one should apply good survey design practices, adequate pretesting or pilot testing of the instrument, and formal tests for validity and reliability. An example of good Web-based eHealth survey design guidelines is the Checklist for Reporting Results of Internet electronic-Surveys (cherries) by Eysenbach (2004). The checklist has eight item categories and 31 individual items that can be used by authors to ensure quality design and reporting of their survey studies.

Adherence to Reporting Standards

Currently there are no universally accepted guidelines or standards for reporting survey studies. In the field of management information systems (mis), Grover, Lee, and Durand (1993) published nine ideal survey methodological attributes for analyzing the quality of mis survey research. In their review of ideal survey methodological attributes, Ju, Chen, Sun, and Wu (2006) found two frequent problems in survey studies published in three top mis journals to be the failure to perform statistical tests for non-response errors and not using multiple data collection methods. In healthcare, Kelly, Clark, Brown, and Sitzia (2003) published a checklist of seven key points to be covered when reporting survey studies. They are listed as follows:

1. Explain the purpose of the study with explicit mention of the research question.
2. Explain why the research is needed and mention previous work to provide context.
3. Provide detail on how study was done that covers: the method and rationale; the instrument with its psychometric properties and references to original development/testing; sample selection and data collection processes.
4. Describe and justify the analytical methods used.
5. Present the results in a concise and factual manner.
6. Interpret and discuss the findings.
7. Present conclusions and recommendations.

Bassi, Lau, and Lesperance (2012) published a survey-based study on the perceived impact of EMR in physician office practices. In the review they used the 9-item assessment tool developed by Grover and colleagues (1993) to appraise the reporting quality of 19 emr survey studies. Using the 9-item tool a score from 0 to 1 was assigned depending on whether the attribute was present or absent, giving a maximum score of 9. Of the 19 survey studies appraised, the quality scores ranged from 0.5 to 8. Over half of the studies did not include a data collection method, the instrument and its validation with respect to pretesting or pilot testing, and non-respondent testing. Only two studies scored 7 or higher which suggested the reporting of the 19 published emr survey studies was highly variable. The criteria used in the 9-item tool are listed as.

1. Report the approach used to randomize or select samples.
2. Report a profile of the sample frame.
3. Report characteristics of the respondents.
4. Use a combination of personal, telephone and mail data collection methods.
5. Append the whole or part of the questionnaire in the publication.
6. Adopt a validated instrument or perform a validity or reliability analysis.
7. Perform an instrument pretest.
8. Report on the response rate.
9. Perform a statistical test to justify the loss of data from non-respondents.

Questionnaires

Questionnaires are the most commonly used tool in survey research. However, the results of a particular survey are worthless if the questionnaire is written inadequately.[3] Questionnaires should produce valid and reliable demographic variable measures and should yield valid and reliable individual disparities that self-report scales generate.

Questionnaires as tools

A variable category that is often measured in survey research are demographic variables, which are used to depict the characteristics of the people surveyed in the sample. Demographic variables include such measures as ethnicity, socioeconomic status, race, and age. Surveys often assess the preferences and attitudes of individuals, and many employ self-report scales to measure people's opinions and judgments about different items presented on a scale. Self-report scales are also used to examine the disparities among people on scale items. These self-report scales, which are usually presented in questionnaire form, are one of the most used instruments in psychology, and thus it is important that the measures be constructed carefully, while also being reliable and valid.

Reliability and validity of self-report measures

Reliable measures of self-report are defined by their consistency. Thus, a reliable self-report measure produces consistent results every time it is executed. A test's reliability can be measured a few ways. First, one can calculate a test-retest reliability. Test-retest reliability entails conducting the same questionnaire on a large sample at two different times. For the questionnaire to be considered reliable, people in the sample do not have to score identically on each test, but rather their position in the score distribution should be similar for both the test and the retest. Self-report measures will generally be more reliable when they have many items measuring a construct. Furthermore, measurements will be more reliable when the factor being measured has greater variability among the individuals in the sample that are being tested. Finally, there will be greater reliability when instructions for the completion of the questionnaire are clear and when there are limited distractions in the testing environment. Contrastingly, a questionnaire is valid if what it measures is what it had originally planned to measure. Construct validity of a measure is the degree to which it measures the theoretical construct that it was originally supposed to measure.

Composing a questionnaire

Six steps can be employed to construct a questionnaire that will produce reliable and valid results. First, one must decide what kind of information should be collected. Second, one must decide how to conduct the questionnaire. Thirdly, one must construct a first draft of the questionnaire. Fourth, the questionnaire should be revised. Next, the questionnaire should be pretested. Finally, the questionnaire should be edited and the procedures for its use should be specified.

Guidelines for the effective wording of questions

The way that a question is phrased can have a large impact on how a research participant will answer the question. Thus, survey researchers must be conscious of their wording when writing survey questions. It is important for researchers to keep in mind that different individuals, cultures, and subcultures can interpret certain words and phrases differently from one another. There are two different types of questions that survey researchers use when writing a questionnaire: free response questions and closed questions. Free response questions are open-ended, whereas closed questions are usually multiple choice. Free response questions are beneficial because they allow the responder greater flexibility, but they are also very difficult to record and score, requiring extensive coding. Contrastingly, closed questions can be scored and coded more easily, but they diminish expressivity and spontaneity of the responder. In general, the vocabulary of the questions should be very simple and direct, and most should be less than twenty words. Each question should be edited for "readability" and should avoid leading or loaded questions. Finally, if multiple items are being used to measure one construct, the wording of some of the items should be worded in the opposite direction to evade response bias.

A respondent's answer to an open-ended question can be coded into a response scale afterwards, or analysed using more qualitative methods.

Order of questions

Survey researchers should carefully construct the order of questions in a questionnaire. For questionnaires that are self-administered, the most interesting questions should be at the beginning of the questionnaire to catch the respondent's attention, while demographic questions should be near the end. Contrastingly, if a survey is being administered over the telephone or in person, demographic questions should be administered at the beginning of the interview to boost the respondent's confidence. Another reason to be mindful of question order may cause a survey response effect in which one question may affect how people respond to subsequent questions as a result of priming.

Nonresponse reduction

The following ways have been recommended for reducing nonresponse in telephone and face-to-face surveys:

- Advance letter. A short letter is sent in advance to inform the sampled respondents about the upcoming survey. The style of the letter should be personalized but not overdone. First, it announces that a phone call will be made, or an interviewer wants to make an appointment to do the survey face-to-face. Second, the research topic will be described. Last, it allows both an expression of the surveyor's appreciation of cooperation and an opening to ask questions on the survey.
- Training. The interviewers are thoroughly trained in how to ask respondents questions, how to work with computers and making schedules for callbacks to respondents who were not reached.
- Short introduction. The interviewer should always start with a short introduction about him or herself. She/he should give her name, the institute she is working for, the length of the interview and goal of the interview. Also it can be useful to make clear that you are not selling anything: this has been shown to lead to a slightly higher responding rate.
- Respondent-friendly survey questionnaire. The questions asked must be clear, non-offensive and easy to respond to for the subjects under study.
- Brevity is also often cited as increasing response rate. A 1996 literature review found mixed evidence to support this claim for both written and verbal surveys, concluding that other factors may often be more important. A 2010 study looking at 100,000 online surveys found response rate dropped by about 3% at 10 questions and about 6% at 20 questions, with drop-off slowing (for example, only 10% reduction at 40 questions). Other studies showed that quality of response degraded toward the end of long surveys.
- Some researchers have also discussed the recipient's role or profession as a potential factor affecting how nonresponse is managed. For example, faxes are not commonly used to distribute surveys, but in a recent study were sometimes preferred by pharmacists, since they frequently receive faxed prescriptions at work but may not always have access to a generally-addressed piece of mail.

Interviewer effects

Survey methodologists have devoted much effort to determining the extent to which interviewee responses are affected by physical characteristics of the interviewer. Main interviewer traits that have been demonstrated to influence survey responses are race, gender, and relative body weight (BMI). These interviewer effects are particularly operant when questions are related to the interviewer trait. Hence, race of interviewer has been shown to affect responses to measures regarding racial attitudes, interviewer sex responses to questions involving gender issues, and interviewer BMI answers to eating and dieting-related questions. While interviewer effects have been investigated mainly for face-to-face surveys, they have also been shown to exist for interview modes with no visual contact, such as telephone surveys and in video-enhanced web surveys. The explanation typically provided for interviewer effects is social desirability bias: survey participants may attempt to project a positive self-image in an effort to conform to the norms they attribute to the interviewer asking questions. Interviewer effects are one example survey response effects.

Case Examples

Clinical Informatics Governance for EHR in Nursing

Collins, Alexander, and Moss (2015) conducted an exploratory survey study to understand clinical informatics (ci) governance for nursing and to propose a governance model with recommended roles, partnerships and councils for ehr adoption and optimization. The study is summarized below.

- Setting – Integrated healthcare systems in the United States with at least one acute care hospital that had pioneered enterprise-wide ehr implementation projects and had reached the Health Information Management Systems Society (HIMSS) Analytics' EMR Adoption Model (EMRAM) level 6 or greater, or were undergoing enterprise-wide integration, standardization and optimization of existing EHR systems across sites.

- Population and samples – Nursing informatics leaders in the role of an executive in an integrated healthcare system who could offer their perspective and lessons learned in their organization's clinical and nursing informatics governance structure and its evolution. The sampling frame was the himss Analytics database that contains detailed information on most u.s. healthcare organizations and their health it status.
- Design – A cross-sectional survey conducted through semi-structured telephone interviews with probing questions.
- Measures – The survey had four sections: (a) organizational characteristics; (b) participant characteristics; (c) governance structure; and (d) lessons learned. Questions on governance covered decision-making, committees, collaboration, roles, and facilitators/barriers for success in overall and nursing-specific CI governance.
- Analysis – Grounded theory techniques of open, axial and selective coding were used to identify overlapping themes on governance structures and ci roles. Data were collected until thematic saturation in open coding was reached. The ci structures of each organization were drawn, compared and synthesized into a proposed model of ci roles, partnerships and councils for nursing. Initial coding was independently validated among the researchers and group consensus was used in thematic coding to develop the model.
- Results – Twelve nursing executives (made up of six chief nursing information officers, four directors of nursing informatics, one chief information officer, and one chief CI officer) were interviewed by phone. For analysis 128 open codes were created and organized into 18 axial coding categories where further selective coding led to four high-level themes for the proposed model. The four themes (with lessons learned included) identified as important are: inter-professional partnerships; defining role-based levels of practice and competence; integration into existing clinical infrastructure; and governance as an evolving process.
- Conclusion – The proposed CI governance model can help understand, shape and standardize roles, competencies and structures in CI practices for nursing, as well as be extended to other domains.

Primary Care EMR Adoption, Use and Impacts

Paré et al. (2013) conducted a descriptive survey study to examine the adoption, use and impacts of primary care EMRs in a Canadian province. The study is summarized below.

1. Setting – Primary care clinics in the Canadian Province of Quebec that had adopted electronic medical records under the provincial government's emr adoption incentive and accreditation programs.
2. Population and samples – The population consisted of family physicians as members of the Quebec Federation of General Practitioners that practice in primary care clinics in the province. The sample had three types of physician respondents that: (a) had not adopted emr (type-1); (b) had emr in their clinic but were not using it to support their practice (type-2); or (c) used emr in their clinic to support their practice (type-3).
3. Design – A cross-sectional survey in the form of a pretested online questionnaire in English and French accessible via a secure website. E-mail invitations were sent to all members followed by an e-mail reminder. With a sampling frame of 9,166 active family physicians in Quebec, 370 responses would be needed to obtain a representative sample with a 95% confidence interval and a margin of error of ±5%.
4. Measures – For all three respondent types the measures were clinic and socio-demographic profiles and comments. For type-2 and type-3 respondents, the measures were emr brand and year of implementation. For type-1 the measures were barriers and intent to adopt emr. For type-2 the measures were reasons and influencing factors for not using emr, and intent to use emr in future. For type-3 the measures were emr use experience, level and satisfaction, ease of use with advanced EMR features, and individual/organizational impacts associated with emr use.
5. Analysis – Descriptive statistics in frequencies, per cent and mean Likert scores were used on selected measures. Key analyses included comparison of frequencies by: socio-demographic and clinic profiles; barrier and adoption intent; emr feature availability and use; and comparison of mean Likert scores for satisfaction and individual and organizational impacts. Individual impacts included perceived efficiency, quality of care and work satisfaction. Organizational impacts included effects on clinical staff, the clinic's financial position, and clients.
6. Results – Of 4,845 invited physicians, 780 responded to the survey (16% response rate) that was representative of the population. Just over half of

emr users reported the high cost and complexity in emr acquisition and deployment as the main barriers. Half of non-users reported their clinics intended to deploy emr in the next year. emr users made extensive use of basic emr features such as clinical notes, lab results and scheduling, but few used clinical decision support and data sharing features. For work organization, emrs addressed logistical issues with paper systems. For care quality, EMRs improved the quality of clinical notes and safety of care provided but not clinical decision-making. For care continuity, emrs had poor ability to transfer clinical data among providers.

7. Conclusion – emr impacts related to a physician's experience where the perceived benefits were tied to the duration of emr use. Health organizations should continue to certify emr products to ensure alignment with the provincial EHR.

Nurses' Acceptance of Barcoded Medication Administration Technology

Holden and colleagues (2012) conducted an explanatory survey study to identify predictors of nurses' acceptance of barcoded medication administration (BCMA) in a USA pediatric hospital. The study is summarized below.

1. Setting – A 236-bed free-standing, a pharmacy information system and automated medication-The hospital also had COPE, a pharmacy information system and automated medication-dispensing units.
2. Population and Sample – The population consisted of registered nurses that worked at least 24 hours per week at the hospital. The sample consisted of nurses from three care units that had used bcma for three or more months.
3. Design – A cross-sectional paper survey with reminders was conducted to test the hypothesis that bcma acceptance would be best predicted by a larger set of contextualized variables than the base variables in the Technology Acceptance Model (tam). A multi-item scales survey instrument, validated in previous studies with several added items, was used. The psychometric properties of the survey scales were pretested with 16 non-study nurses.

4. Measures – Seven BCMA-related perceptions: ease of use, usefulness for the job, non-specific social influence, training, technical support, usefulness for patient care, and social influence from patients/families. Responses were 7-point scales from not-at-all to a-great-deal. Also tracked were variables for age in five categories, as well as experience measured as job tenure in years and months. Two bcma acceptance variables: behavioural intention to use and satisfaction.
5. Analysis – Regression of all subsets of perceptions to identify the best predictors of bcma acceptance using five goodness-of-fit indicators (i.e., R2, root mean square error, Mallow's Cp statistics, Akaike information criterion, and Bayesian information criterion). An a priori α criterion of 0.05 was used and 95% confidence intervals were computed around parameter estimates.
6. Results – Ninety-four of 202 nurses returned a survey (46.5% response rate) but 11 worked less than 24 hours per week and were excluded, leaving a final sample of 83 respondents. Nurses perceived moderate ease of use and low usefulness of bcma. They perceived moderate or higher social influence to use bcma, and were moderately positive about bcma training and technical support. Behavioural intention to use bcma was high but satisfaction was low. Behavioural intention to use bcma was best predicted by perceived ease of use, non-specific social influence and usefulness for patient care (56% variance explained). Satisfaction was best predicted by perceived ease of use, usefulness for patient care and social influence from patients/families (76% variances explained).
7. Conclusion – Predicting BCMA acceptance benefited from using a larger set of perceptions and adapting variables.

XI

Evaluation of a Health System: Methods

Introduction

In health system evaluation, comparative studies aim to find out whether group differences in health system adoption make a difference in important outcomes. These groups may differ in their composition, the type of system in use, and the setting where they work over a given time duration. The comparisons are to determine whether significant differences exist for some predefined measures between these groups, while controlling for as many of the conditions as possible such as the composition, system, setting and duration. According to the typology by Friedman and Wyatt (2006), comparative studies take on an objective view where events such as the use and effect of an eHealth system can be defined, measured and compared through a set of variables to prove or disprove a hypothesis. For comparative studies, the design options are experimental versus observational and prospective versus retrospective. The quality of comparative studies depends on such aspects of methodological design as the choice of variables, sample size, sources of bias, confounders, and adherence to quality and reporting guidelines.

In this chapter we will focus on experimental studies as one type of comparative study and their methodological considerations that have been reported in the eHealth literature. Also included are three case examples to show how these studies are done.

Types of Comparative Studies

Experimental studies are one type of comparative study where a sample of participants is identified and assigned to different conditions for a given time duration, then compared for differences. An example is a hospital with two care units where one is assigned a COPE system to process medication orders electronically while the other continues its usual practice without a CPOE. The participants in the unit assigned to the CPOE are called the intervention group and those assigned to usual practice are the control group. The comparison can be performance or outcome focused, such as the ratio of correct orders processed or the occurrence of adverse drug events in the two groups during the given time period. Experimental studies can take on a randomized or non-randomized design. These are described below.

Randomized Experiments

In a randomized design, the participants are randomly assigned to two or more groups using a known randomization technique such as a random number table. The design is prospective in nature since the groups are assigned concurrently, after which the intervention is applied then measured and compared. Three types of experimental designs seen in eHealth evaluation are described below (Friedman & Wyatt, 2006; Zwarenstein & Treweek, 2009).

Randomized controlled trials (RCTs)

In RCTs participants are randomly assigned to an intervention or a control group. The randomization can occur at the patient, provider or organization level, which is known as the unit of allocation. For instance, at the patient level one can randomly assign half of the patients to receive EMR reminders while the other half do not. At the provider level, one can assign half of the providers to receive the reminders while the other half continues with their usual practice. At the organization level, such as a multisite hospital, one can randomly assign emr reminders to some of the sites but not others.

Cluster randomized controlled trials (CRCTs)

In CRCTs, clusters of participants are randomized rather than by individual participant since they are found in naturally occurring groups such as living in the same communities. For instance, clinics in one city may be randomized as a cluster to receive EMR reminders while clinics in another city continue their usual practice.

Pragmatic trials

Unlike RCTs that seek to find out if an intervention such as a CPOE system works under ideal conditions, pragmatic trials are designed to find out if the intervention works under usual conditions. The goal is to make the design and findings relevant to and practical for decision-makers to apply in usual settings. As such, pragmatic trials have few criteria for selecting study participants, flexibility in implementing the intervention, usual practice as the comparator, the same compliance and follow-up intensity as usual practice, and outcomes that are relevant to decision-makers.

Non-randomized Experiments

Non-randomized design is used when it is neither feasible nor ethical to randomize participants into groups for comparison. It is sometimes referred to as a quasi-experimental design. The design can involve the use of prospective or retrospective data from the same or different participants as the control group. Three types of non-randomized designs are described as follows:

Intervention group only with pre-test and post-test design

This design involves only one group where a pretest or baseline measure is taken as the control period, the intervention is implemented, and a post-test measure is taken as the intervention period for comparison. For example, one can compare the rates of medication errors before and after the implementation of a CPOE system in a hospital. To increase study quality, one can add a second pretest period to decrease the probability that the pretest and post-test difference is due to chance, such as an unusually low medication error rate in the first pretest period. Other ways to increase study quality include adding an unrelated outcome such as patient case-mix that should not be affected, removing the intervention to see if the difference remains, and removing then re-implementing the intervention to see if the differences vary accordingly.

Intervention and control groups with post-test design

This design involves two groups where the intervention is implemented in one group and compared with a second group without the intervention, based on a post-test measure from both groups. For example, one can implement a CPOE system in one care unit as the intervention group with a second unit as the control group and compare the post-test medication error rates in both units over six months. To increase study quality, one can add one or more pretest periods to both groups, or implement the intervention to the control group at a later time to measure for similar but delayed effects.

Interrupted time series (ITs) design

In its design, multiple measures are taken from one group in equal time intervals, interrupted by the implementation of the intervention. The multiple pretest and post-test measures decrease the probability that the differences detected are due to chance or unrelated effects. An example is to take six consecutive monthly medication error rates as the pretest measures, implement the CPOE system, then take another six consecutive monthly medication error rates as the post-test measures for comparison in error rate differences over 12 months. To increase study quality, one may add a concurrent control group for comparison to be more convinced that the intervention produced the change.

Process

The quality of comparative studies is dependent on their internal and external validity. Internal validity refers to the extent to which conclusions can be drawn correctly from the study setting, participants, intervention, measures, analysis and interpretations. External validity refers to the extent to which the conclusions can be generalized to other settings. The major factors that influence validity are described below.

Choice of Variables

Variables are specific measurable features that can influence validity. In comparative studies, the choice of dependent and independent variables and whether they are categorical and/or continuous in values can affect the type of questions, study design and analysis to be considered. These are described as follows:

- *Dependent variables* – This refers to outcomes of interest; they are also known as outcome variables. An example is the rate of medication errors as an outcome in determining whether CPOE can improve patient safety.
- *Independent variables* – This refers to variables that can explain the measured values of the dependent variables. For instance, the characteristics of the setting, participants and intervention can influence the effects of CPOE.
- *Categorical variables* – This refers to variables with measured values in discrete categories or levels. Examples are the type of providers (e.g., nurses, physicians and pharmacists), the presence or absence of a disease, and pain scale (e.g., 0 to 10 in increments of 1). Categorical variables are analyzed using non-parametric methods such as chi-square and odds ratio.

- *Continuous variables* – This refers to variables that can take on infinite values within an interval limited only by the desired precision. Examples are blood pressure, heart rate and body temperature. Continuous variables are analyzed using parametric methods such as *t*-test, analysis of variance or multiple regression.

Sample Size

Sample size is the number of participants to include in a study. It can refer to patients, providers or organizations depending on how the unit of allocation is defined. There are four parts to calculating sample size. They are described as follows:

- *Significance level* – This refers to the probability that a positive finding is due to chance alone. It is usually set at 0.05, which means having a less than 5% chance of drawing a false positive conclusion.
- *Power* – This refers to the ability to detect the true effect based on a sample from the population. It is usually set at 0.8, which means having at least an 80% chance of drawing a correct conclusion.
- *Effect size* – This refers to the minimal clinically relevant difference that can be detected between comparison groups. For continuous variables, the effect is a numerical value such as a 10-kilogram weight difference between two groups. For categorical variables, it is a percentage such as a 10% difference in medication error rates.
- *Variability* – This refers to the population variance of the outcome of interest, which is often unknown and is estimated by way of standard deviation (sd) from pilot or previous studies for continuous outcome.
- Sample Size Equations for Comparing Two Groups with Continuous and Categorical Outcome Variables.

An example of sample size calculation for an RCT to examine the effect of CDS on improving systolic blood pressure of hypertensive patients is provided in the Appendix. Refer to the Biomath website from Columbia University for a simple Web-based sample ssize/powercalculator.

Sources of Bias

There are five common sources of biases in comparative studies. They are selection, performance, detection, attrition and reporting biases. These biases, and the ways to minimize them, are described as follows

- *Selection or allocation bias* – This refers to differences between the compositions of comparison groups in terms of the response to the intervention. An example is having sicker or older patients in the control group than those in the intervention group when evaluating the effect of EMR reminders. To reduce selection bias, one can apply randomization and concealment when assigning participants to groups and ensure their compositions are comparable at baseline.
- *Performance bias* – This refers to differences between groups in the care they received, aside from the intervention being evaluated. An example is the different ways by which reminders are triggered and used within and across groups such as electronic, paper and phone reminders for patients and providers. To reduce performance bias, one may standardize the intervention and blind participants from knowing whether an intervention was received and which intervention was received.
- *Detection or measurement bias* – This refers to differences between groups in how outcomes are determined. An example is where outcome assessors pay more attention to outcomes of patients known to be in the intervention group. To reduce detection bias, one may blind assessors from participants when measuring outcomes and ensure the same timing for assessment across groups.
- *Attrition bias* – This refers to differences between groups in ways that participants are withdrawn from the study. An example is the low rate of participant response in the intervention group despite having received reminders for follow-up care. To reduce attrition bias, one needs to acknowledge the dropout rate and analyze data according to an intent-to-treat principle (i.e., include data from those who dropped out in the analysis).
- *Reporting bias* – This refers to differences between reported and unreported findings. Examples include biases in publication, time lag, citation, language and outcome reporting depending on the nature and direction of the results. To reduce reporting bias, one may make the study protocol available with all pre-specified outcomes and report all expected outcomes in published results.

Confounders

Confounders are factors other than the intervention of interest that can distort the effect because they are associated with both the intervention and the outcome. For instance, in a study to demonstrate whether the adoption of a medication order entry system led to lower medication costs, there can be a number of potential confounders that can affect the outcome. These may include severity of illness of the patients, provider knowledge and experience with the system, and hospital policy on prescribing medications. Another example is the evaluation of the effect of an antibiotic reminder system on the rate of postoperative deep venous thrombosis (DVTs). The confounders can be general improvements in clinical practice during the study such as prescribing patterns and post-operative care that are not related to the reminders. To control for confounding effects, one may consider the use of matching, stratification and modelling. Matching involves the selection of similar groups with respect to their composition and behaviours. Stratification involves the division of participants into subgroups by selected variables, such as comorbidity index to control for severity of illness. Modelling involves the use of statistical techniques such as multiple regression to adjust for the effects of specific variables such as age, sex and/or severity of illness.

Guidelines on Quality and Reporting

There are guidelines on the quality and reporting of comparative studies. The GRADE (Grading of Recommendations Assessment, Development and Evaluation) guidelines provide explicit criteria for rating the quality of studies in randomized trials and observational studies. The extended CONSORT (Consolidated Standards of Reporting Trials) Statements for non-pharmacologic trials, pragmatic trials, and eHealth interventions provide reporting guidelines for randomized trials.

The GRADE guidelines offer a system of rating quality of evidence in systematic reviews and guidelines. In this approach, to support estimates of intervention effects RCTs start as high-quality evidence and observational studies as low-quality evidence. For each outcome in a study, five factors may rate down the quality of evidence. The final quality of evidence for each outcome would fall into one of high, moderate, low, and very low quality. These factors are listed as follows:

- *Design limitations* – For RCTs they cover the lack of allocation concealment, lack of blinding, large loss to follow-up, trial stopped early or selective outcome reporting.
- *Inconsistency of results* – Variations in outcomes due to unexplained heterogeneity. An example is the unexpected variation of effects across subgroups of patients by severity of illness in the use of preventive care

reminders.

- *Indirectness of evidence* – Reliance on indirect comparisons due to restrictions in study populations, intervention, comparator or outcomes. An example is the 30-day readmission rate as a surrogate outcome for quality of computer-supported emergency care in hospitals.
- *Imprecision of results* – Studies with small sample size and few events typically would have wide confidence intervals and are considered of low quality.
- *Publication bias* – The selective reporting of results at the individual study level is already covered under design limitations, but is included here for completeness as it is relevant when rating quality of evidence across studies in systematic reviews.

The original CONSORT Statement has 22 checklist items for reporting RCTs. For non-pharmacologic trials extensions have been made to 11 items. For pragmatic trials extensions have been made to eight items. These items are listed below. For further details, readers can refer to the consort website.

1. *Title and abstract* – one item on the means of randomization used.
2. *Introduction* – one item on background, rationale, and problem addressed by the intervention.
3. *Methods* – 10 items on participants, interventions, objectives, outcomes, sample size, randomization (sequence generation, allocation concealment, implementation), blinding (masking), and statistical methods.
4. *Results* – seven items on participant flow, recruitment, baseline data, and numbers analyzed, outcomes and estimation, ancillary analyses, adverse events.
5. *Discussion* – three items on interpretation, generalizability, overall evidence.

The CONSORT Statement for eHealth interventions describes the relevance of the consort recommendations to the design and reporting of eHealth studies with an emphasis on Internet-based interventions for direct use by patients, such as online health information resources, decision aides and PHRs. Of particular importance is the need to clearly define the intervention components, their role in the overall care process, target population, implementation process, primary and secondary outcomes, denominators for outcome analyses, and real world potential.

Case Examples

Pragmatic RCT in Vascular Risk Decision Support

Holbrook et al., 2011 conducted a pragmatic RCT to examine the effects of a CDS intervention on vascular care and outcomes for older adults. The study is summarized below.

- *Setting* – Community-based primary care practices with EMRs in one Canadian province.
- *Participants* – English-speaking patients 55 years of age or older with diagnosed vascular disease, no cognitive impairment and not living in a nursing home, who had a provider visit in the past 12 months.
- *Intervention* – A Web-based individualized vascular tracking and advice CDS system for eight top vascular risk factors and two diabetic risk factors, for use by both providers and patients and their families. Providers and staff could update the patient's profile at any time and the CDS algorithm ran nightly to update recommendations and colour highlighting used in the tracker interface. Intervention patients had Web access to the tracker, a print version mailed to them prior to the visit, and telephone support on advice.
- *Design* – Pragmatic, one-year, two-arm, multicentre RCT, with randomization upon patient consent by phone, using an allocation-concealed online program. Randomization was by patient with stratification by provider using a block size of six. Trained reviewers examined emr data and conducted patient telephone interviews to collect risk factors, vascular history, and vascular events. Providers completed questionnaires on the intervention at study end. Patients had final 12-month lab checks on urine albumin, low-density lipoprotein cholesterol, and A1C levels.
- *Outcomes* – Primary outcome was based on change in process composite score (PCS) computed as the sum of frequency-weighted process score for each of the eight main risk factors with a maximum score of 27. The process was considered met if a risk factor had been checked. PCS was measured at baseline and study end with the difference as the individual primary outcome scores. The main secondary outcome was a clinical composite score (CCS) based on the same eight risk factors compared in two ways: a comparison of the mean number of clinical variables on target and the percentage of patients with improvement between the

two groups. Other secondary outcomes were actual vascular event rates, individual pcs and ccs components, ratings of usability, continuity of care, patient ability to manage vascular risk, and quality of life using the EuroQol five dimensions questionnaire (eq-5d).

- *Analysis* – 1,100 patients were needed to achieve 90% power in detecting a one-point PCS difference between groups with a standard deviation of five points, two-tailed *t*-test for mean difference at 5% significance level, and a withdrawal rate of 10%. The PCS, CCS and eq-5d scores were analyzed using a generalized estimating equation accounting for clustering within providers. Descriptive statistics and $\chi 2$ tests or exact tests were done with other outcomes.
- *Findings* – 1,102 patients and 49 providers enrolled in the study. The intervention group with 545 patients had significant PCS improvement with a difference of 4.70 ($p < .001$) on a 27-point scale. The intervention group also had significantly higher odds of rating improvements in their continuity of care (4.178, $p < .001$) and ability to improve their vascular health (3.07, $p < .001$). There was no significant change in vascular events, clinical variables and quality of life. Overall the CDS intervention led to reduced vascular risks but not to improved clinical outcomes in a one-year follow-up.

Non-randomized Experiment in Antibiotic Prescribing in Primary Care

Mainous, Lambourne, and Nietert (2013) conducted a prospective non-randomized trial to examine the impact of a CDS system on antibiotic prescribing for acute respiratory infections (ARIS) in primary care. The study is summarized below.

- *Setting* – A primary care research network in the United States whose members use a common EMR and pool data quarterly for quality improvement and research studies.
- *Participants* – An intervention group with nine practices across nine states, and a control group with 61 practices.
- *Intervention* – Point-of-care CDS tool as customizable progress note templates based on existing EMR features. cds recommendations reflect Centre for Disease Control and Prevention (CDC guidelines based on a patient's predominant presenting symptoms and age. CDS was used to assist in ARI diagnosis, prompt antibiotic use, record diagnosis and

treatment decisions, and access printable patient and provider education resources from the CDC.

- *Design* – The intervention group received a multi-method intervention to facilitate provider CDS adoption that included quarterly audit and feedback, best practice dissemination meetings, academic detailing site visits, performance review and CDS training. The control group did not receive information on the intervention, the cds or education. Baseline data collection was for three months with follow-up of 15 months after CDS implementation.
- *Outcomes* – The outcomes were frequency of inappropriate prescribing during an ARI episode, broad-spectrum antibiotic use and diagnostic shift. Inappropriate prescribing was computed by dividing the number of ARI episodes with diagnoses in the inappropriate category that had an antibiotic prescription by the total number of ARI episodes with diagnosis for which antibiotics are inappropriate. Broad-spectrum antibiotic use was computed by all ARI episodes with a broad-spectrum antibiotic prescription by the total number of ARI episodes with an antibiotic prescription. Antibiotic drift was computed in two ways: dividing the number of ARI episodes with diagnoses where antibiotics are appropriate by the total number of ARI episodes with an antibiotic prescription; and dividing the number of ARI episodes where antibiotics were inappropriate by the total number of ARI episodes. Process measure included frequency of CDS template use and whether the outcome measures differed by CDS usage.
- *Analysis* – Outcomes were measured quarterly for each practice, weighted by the number of ARI episodes during the quarter to assign greater weight to practices with greater numbers of relevant episodes and to periods with greater numbers of relevant episodes. Weighted means and 95% CIs were computed separately for adult and pediatric (less than 18 years of age) patients for each time period for both groups. Baseline means in outcome measures were compared between the two groups using weighted independent-sample *t*-tests. Linear mixed models were used to compare changes over the 18-month period. The models included time, intervention status, and were adjusted for practice characteristics such as specialty, size, and region and baseline aris. Random practice effects were included to account for clustering of repeated measures on practices over time. *P*-values of less than 0.05 were considered significant.

- *Findings* – For adult patients, inappropriate prescribing in ARI episodes declined more among the intervention group (-0.6%) than the control group (4.2%) ($p = 0.03$), and prescribing of broad-spectrum antibiotics declined by 16.6% in the intervention group versus an increase of 1.1% in the control group ($p < 0.0001$). For pediatric patients, there was a similar decline of 19.7% in the intervention group versus an increase of 0.9% in the control group ($p < 0.0001$). In summary, the CDS had a modest effect in reducing inappropriate prescribing for adults, but had a substantial effect in reducing the prescribing of broad-spectrum antibiotics in adult and pediatric patients.

Interrupted Time Series on EHR Impact in Nursing Care

Dowding, Turley, and Garrido (2012) conducted a prospective its study to examine the impact of EHR implementation on nursing care processes and outcomes. The study is summarized below.

- *Setting* – Kaiser Permanente (KP) as a large not-for-profit integrated healthcare organization in the United States.
- *Participants* – 29 KP hospitals in the northern and southern regions of California.
- *Intervention* – An integrated EHR system implemented at all hospitals with COPE, nursing documentation and risk assessment tools. The nursing component for risk assessment documentation of pressure ulcers and falls was consistent across hospitals and developed by clinical nurses and informaticists by consensus.
- *Design* – ITs design with monthly data on pressure ulcers and quarterly data on fall rates and risk collected over seven years between 2003 and 2009. All data were collected at the unit level for each hospital.
- *Outcomes* – Process measures were the proportion of patients with a fall risk assessment done and the proportion with a hospital-acquired pressure ulcer (HAPU) risk assessment done within 24 hours of admission. Outcome measures were fall and HAPU rates as part of the unit-level nursing care process and nursing sensitive outcome data collected routinely for all California hospitals. Fall rate was defined as the number of unplanned descents to the floor per 1,000 patient days, and HAPU rate was the percentage of patients with stages i-iv or unstageable ulcer on the day of data collection.

- *Analysis* – Fall and HAPU risk data were synchronized using the month in which the EHR was implemented at each hospital as time zero and aggregated across hospitals for each time period. Multivariate regression analysis was used to examine the effect of time, region and EHR.
- *Findings* – The EHR was associated with significant increase in document rates for HAPU risk (2.21; 95% CI 0.67 to 3.75) and non-significant increase for fall risk (0.36; -3.58 to 4.30). The EHR was associated with 13% decrease in HAPU rates (-0.76; -1.37 to -0.16) but no change in fall rates (-0.091; -0.29 to 011). Hospital region was a significant predictor of variation for HAPU (0.72; 0.30 to 1.14) and fall rates (0.57; 0.41 to 0.72). During the study period, HAPU rates decreased significantly (-0.16; -0.20 to -0.13) but not fall rates (0.0052; -0.01 to 0.02). In summary, EHR implementation was associated with a reduction in the number of HAPUs but not patient falls, and changes over time and hospital region also affected outcomes.

XII

EPIDEMOLOGY: OVERVIEW

Introduction

Epidemiology is "the study of the distribution and determinants of diseases and injuries in human populations." The term epidemiology is derived from Greek words that can be translated into the phrase "the study of that which is upon the people." The goal of epidemiology is to limit disease, injury, and death in a community by intervening to prevent or limit outbreaks or epidemics of disease and injury. This is accomplished by describing outbreaks and designing studies to analyze them and validate new approaches to prevention, control, and treatment. Through these practices, epidemiologists contribute to our knowledge of how diseases begin and spread through populations, and how they can be prevented, controlled, and treated.

A question may be raised, how many cases are required before a disease outbreak is considered an epidemic—10 cases? 100 cases? 1,000 cases? The answer is that it depends upon the disease and the population, but an unexpectedly large number of cases of a disease in a particular population at a particular time and place can be considered an epidemic. Some recent epidemics in the United States are presented in. The question might be asked, what are diseases called that occur regularly in a population but are not epidemic? These diseases are referred to as endemic diseases. Whether a disease is an epidemic or endemic depends on the disease and the population. Heart disease is endemic in America, while in many regions of equatorial Africa, malaria is endemic. While an epidemiologist studies outbreaks of disease, injury, and death in human populations (epidemics), an epizootiology studies disease outbreaks in animal populations (epizootics). Some diseases, such as bubonic plague and St. Louis encephalitis, may begin as epizootics but later become epidemics. When both animals and humans are involved in a disease outbreak, the term epizoodemic is appropriate. Occasionally, an epidemic will spread over a wide area, perhaps even across an entire continent or around the world. Such a widespread epidemic is termed a pandemic.

For example, the influenza pandemic of 1918. This disease spread from France to Spain and then to England and to the rest of Europe. It then spread to China and West Africa and eventually reached the United States, Australia, and New Zealand. More or less 25 million people died over several years as a result. The recent outbreak of HIV/AIDS is another example of a pandemic. During 2003, an estimated 3 million people died of HIV/AIDS worldwide.

History

If one searches diligently, it is possible to trace the roots of epidemiological thinking back to the "Father of Medicine," Hippocrates, who as early as 300 B.C. suggested a relationship between the occurrence of disease and the physical environment. For example, cases of a disease fitting the description of malaria were found to occur in the vicinity of marshes and swamps. With the fall of the classical civilizations of Greece and Rome and the return of Europe to a belief in spiritual causes of disease, few advances were made in the field of epidemiology. As a result, epidemics continued to occur. There were three waves of plague—one in 542–543, one in 1348–1349, and another in 1664–1665. There were also epidemics of leprosy, smallpox, malaria, and, later, syphilis and yellow fever. Epidemics occurred in the New World as well. One such epidemic of yellow fever struck Philadelphia in 1793, causing the death of 4,044 people. Yellow fever was epidemic again in Philadelphia in 1797, 1798, and in 1803.

Benjamin Rush, a notable physician, was able to trace the causes of yellow fever to the docks where ships arrived from tropical ports. However, his conclusion that the disease was caused by vapors arising from decaying coffee beans in port warehouses was incorrect. He could not have known that yellow fever is caused by a virus and is carried by the yellow fever mosquito, *Aedes aegypti*. These facts were discovered by *Major* **Walter Reed** of the U.S. Army and his associates a century later. In 1849, some 50 years after the yellow fever outbreaks in Philadelphia, cholera became epidemic in London.

Physician, **John Snow**, investigated the outbreak by interviewing numerous victims and their families. He concluded that the source of the epidemic was probably water drawn from a particular communal well located on Broad Street. Snow extinguished the epidemic when he removed the pump handle from the Broad Street pump, thus forcing people to obtain their water elsewhere. John Snow's quashing of the London cholera epidemic in 1849 is a classic example of how epidemiological methods can be used to limit disease and deaths. His achievement was even more remarkable because it occurred 30 years before **Louis Pasteur** proposed his "germ theory of disease."It was not until 1883 that **Robert Koch** discovered the organism that causes cholera, *Vibrio cholerae.*

From its early use for the description and investigation of communicable diseases, epidemiology has developed into a sophisticated field of science. Epidemiological methods are used to evaluate everything from the effectiveness of vaccines to the possible causes of occupational illnesses and unintentional injury deaths. Knowledge of epidemiology is important to the community health worker who wishes to establish the presence of a set of needs or conditions for a particular health service or program or to justify a request for funding. Likewise, epidemiological methods are used to evaluate the effectiveness of programs already in existence and to plan to meet anticipated needs for facilities and personnel.

Epidemological studies

When disease and/or death occurs in unexpected or unacceptable numbers, epidemiologists may carry out investigations. These investigations may be descriptive, analytical, or experimental in nature, depending upon the objectives of the specific study.

Descriptive studies

Descriptive studies seek to describe the extent of an outbreak in regard to person, time, and place. These studies are designed to answer the questions of who, when, and where. To answer the first question, epidemiologists first take a "head count" to determine how many cases of the disease have occurred. At this time, they also try to determine who is ill—children, elders, men, women, or both. The data they gather should permit them to develop a summary of cases by age, sex, race, marital status, and type of employment. To answer the second question (**when**), epidemiologists must determine the time of the onset of illness for each case. The resulting data can be used to prepare an epidemic curve, a graphic display of the cases of the disease by the time or date of the onset of their symptoms. Three types of epidemic curves are commonly used in descriptive studies—secular, seasonal, and single epidemic curves. The secular display of a disease shows the distribution of cases over many years (e.g., cases of paralytic poliomyelitis for the period 1972 to 2002). Secular graphs illustrate the long-term trend of a disease. A graph of the case data by season or month is usually prepared to show cyclical changes in the number of cases of a disease. Cases of arthropod-borne viral infections, for example, peak in the late summer months, following the seasonal rise in populations of the mosquitoes that transmit them.

Epidemic curves for single epidemics vary in appearance with each disease outbreak; however, two classical types exist. The first is the point source epidemic curve. In a point source epidemic, each case can be traced to exposure to the same source—spoiled food, for example. Because an epidemic curve shows cases of the disease by the time or date of the onset of their symptoms, the epidemic curve for a single epidemic can be used to calculate the incubation period, the period of time between exposure to an infectious agent, and the onset of symptoms. The incubation period, together with the symptoms, can often help epidemiologists determine the cause of the disease.

The second type of epidemic curve for a solitary outbreak is a propagated epidemic curve. In this type of epidemic, primary cases appear first at the end of the incubation period following exposure to an infected source. Secondary cases arise after a second incubation period, and they represent exposure to the primary cases; tertiary cases appear even later due to exposure to secondary cases, and so on. Because new cases give rise to more new cases, this type of epidemic is termed a propagated epidemic. Epidemics of communicable diseases like chickenpox follow this pattern.

Finally, epidemiologists must determine where the outbreak occurred. To determine where the illnesses may have originated, the residential address and travel history of each case are recorded. This information provides a geographic distribution of cases and helps to delineate the extent of the outbreak. By plotting cases on a map, along with natural features such as streams and human-made structures such as factories, it is sometimes possible to learn something about the source of the disease. A descriptive study is usually the first epidemiological study carried out on a disease. Detectable patterns of cases may provide investigators with ideas that can lead to a hypothesis about the cause or source of a disease. As important and useful as they are, descriptive studies have limited usefulness. Results from descriptive studies are usually not applicable to outbreaks elsewhere. Also, the investigation of a single epidemic cannot provide information about disease trends. Lastly, with few exceptions, descriptive studies by themselves rarely identify with certainty the cause of an outbreak.

Analytical Studies

Another type of epidemiological study is the analytical study. The purpose of analytical studies is to test hypotheses about relationships between health problems and possible risk factors, factors that increase the probability of disease. While front-line community health workers usually do not conduct analytical studies, it is important that students of community health understand how they are carried out and what kinds of data they generate. Only through such an understanding can those who work in community health interpret the findings of these studies to others in the community, who may then apply the knowledge to improve their own health and that of the community. An example of an analytical study might be one designed to discover whether diabetes (health problem) is associated with obesity (possible risk factor), or whether lung cancer (health problem) is associated with cigarette smoking (possible risk factor). It is important to remember that the associations discovered through analytical epidemiological studies are not always cause-and-effect associations.

There are two types of analytical studies—retrospective and prospective.

Retrospective studies are epidemiological studies that compare people with the disease (cases) to healthy people of similar age, sex, and background (controls), with respect to prior exposure to possible risk factors. These case/control studies are aimed at identifying familial, environmental, or behavioral factors that are more common or more pronounced in the case group than in the control group. Such factors could be associated with the disease under study. For example, epidemiologists might wish to study the factors associated with cervical cancer in women. To carry out this study, epidemiologists would identify a number of women with cervical cancer (cases) and an equal or larger number of healthy women (controls). Medical histories for each group would be obtained and compared. In this hypothetical example, an examination of the history suggests that cigarette smoking is more prevalent in the case group. If exposure to the possible risk factor (smoking) is significantly greater in the cases (of cervical cancer) than in the controls, an association is said to exist. Note that this association may or may not be one of cause and effect. Further studies are usually necessary to confirm initial findings. Retrospective studies almost never prove causation by themselves. Instead, they usually indicate the direction for future studies.

Prospective studies or **cohort studies** are epidemiological studies in which the researcher selects a cohort, a large number of healthy subjects that share a similar experience such as year of birth or high school graduation. Subjects in this cohort are then classified on the basis of their exposure to one or more possible causative factors such as cigarette smoking, dietary habits, or other factors. The entire cohort is then observed for a number of years to determine the rate at which disease develops in each subgroup that was classified by exposure factor. It is important to note the difference in the type of results obtained from retrospective and prospective studies and the advantages and disadvantages of each type of study.

In retrospective studies, results obtained are not true incidence rates because the disease was already present at the beginning of the study; that is, there were cases and controls to begin with, rather than a population-at-risk. For this reason, retrospective studies can only provide a probability statement about the association between factors and disease. This probability statement can be stated mathematically as an odds ratio. The following is a hypothetical example of such a probability statement: Lung cancer patients have a probability of having smoked cigarettes that is 11 times greater than that of the control group. The odds ratio, in this case, is 11:1. In prospective studies, one begins with a population-at-risk, and therefore is able to calculate the risk of developing disease associated with each examined factor.

This relative risk states the relationship between the risk of acquiring the disease in the presence of the risk factor to the risk of acquiring the disease in the absence of the risk factor. For example, a relative risk statement is: Smokers are 11 times more likely to develop lung cancer than nonsmokers. Although prospective studies yield a relative risk, they have three distinct disadvantages:

- Prospective studies are expensive.
- Prospective studies take many years to complete.
- Prospective studies are not very useful for studying rare diseases because the disease may not develop in the cohort.

Retrospective studies, on the other hand, are less expensive to carry out, can be completed more quickly, and are useful for studying rare diseases because one can select the cases. Unfortunately, they cannot yield a true risk for acquiring a disease.

Experimental Studies

Experimental studies are carried out in order to identify the cause of a disease or to determine the effectiveness of a vaccine, therapeutic drug, or surgical procedure. The central feature of experimental studies is the control of variables surrounding the experimental subjects. These subjects may be humans but more often are animals such as laboratory mice, rats, or monkeys. The use of research animals in experimental studies is necessary to determine the safety and effectiveness of new therapeutic agents or medical procedures with minimum risk to human health.

Whether animals or humans are used, every effort is made to reduce unwanted variability associated with the experimental subjects. In the case of animal studies, the variables over which the experimenter may wish to exert control include age, sex, diet, and environmental conditions. In addition to controlling variables, three other principles are essential to properly designed experimental studies—control groups, randomization, and blindness. The use of control groups means that the experimental treatment (intervention) such as drug, vaccine, smoke-free environment, or special diet, is withheld from a portion of the subjects. These subjects belong to the control group, which receives blank doses or treatments, called placebos. In order for a treatment regimen to be considered effective or for a factor to be considered causally related, it must significantly affect the treatment group differently (usually determined using a statistical test) from the control group.

Randomization refers to the practice of assigning subjects to treatments or control groups in a completely random manner. This can be accomplished by assigning numbers to subjects and then having numbers selected randomly. Numbers can be selected randomly from a table of random numbers, by drawing lots, or by using a computer-generated list of random numbers. Thus, each research subject, human or animal, has an equal chance of being placed in the treatment group. Blindness refers to the practice in which the researcher remains uninformed and unaware of the identities of treatment and control groups throughout the period of experimentation and data gathering. This prevents the researcher from looking favorably or unfavorably at the responses of any particular subject or group while gathering data during the experiment. Thus, the researcher can remain unbiased.

When studies involve human subjects, it is important that the subjects also remain uninformed as to whether they have been placed in the treatment group or control (placebo) group. Such a procedure is referred to as double-blind(neither researcher nor subjects know who is receiving the treatment), and it often involves the use of a placebo, such as a saline (salt-water) injection or sugar pill. The use of a placebo prevents subjects from determining by observation whether or not they are receiving treatment. This is important because human thought processes are such that some people begin to feel better if they believe they have received treatment. In order for a vaccine or therapeutic drug to be labeled as effective, it must consistently perform better than a placebo.

Tonnesen and his colleagues studied the effectiveness of a 16-hour nicotine patch on smoking cessation. They used a double-blind randomized design to compare the effects of a nicotine skin patch with those of a placebo skin patch. Subjects were assigned to the active treatment or the placebo according to computer-generated random numbers. There were 145 subjects who received a nicotine patch and 144 who received the placebo. Subjects were scheduled for visits 1, 3, 6, 12, 26, and 52 weeks after the first visit—the day smoking cessation was to begin. The results of this study indicated that there was a significant difference between the effectiveness of the nicotine patch and the placebo patch with regard to smoking cessation. Controlling variables, the use of treatment and control groups, randomization, and blindness are techniques aimed at ensuring objectivity and avoiding bias in experimental studies. Through strict adherence to these principles, researchers hope to achieve experimental results that accurately reflect what occurs in a natural setting.

By carrying out carefully planned descriptive studies, epidemiologists define outbreaks of disease, injury, and death in specific populations and develop hypotheses about the causes of these outbreaks. By designing and carrying out analytical and experimental studies, epidemiologists test these hypotheses.

Classification of diseases

Diseases and health problems can be classified in several meaningful ways. The diseases are often classified by organ or organ system, such as kidney disease, heart disease, respiratory infection, and so on. Another method of classification is by causative agent—viral diseases, chemical poisoning, physical injury, and so forth. In this scheme, causative agents may be biological, chemical, or physical. Biological agents include viruses, rickettsiae, bacteria, protozoa, fungi, and metazoa (multicellular organisms). Chemical agents include drugs, pesticides, industrial chemicals, food additives, air pollutants, and cigarette smoke. Physical agents that can cause injury or disease include various forms of energy such as heat, ultraviolet light, radiation, noise vibrations, and speeding or falling objects. In community health, diseases are usually classified as acute or chronic, or as communicable (infectious) or non-communicable (non-infectious)

Communicable and Noncommunicable Diseases

An important classification system divides diseases into communicable and non-communicable diseases.

Communicable (infectious) diseases are those diseases for which biological agents or their products are the cause and that are transmissible from one individual to another. The disease process begins when the agent is able to lodge and grow or reproduce within the body of the host. The process of lodgment and growth of a microorganism or virus in the host is called infection.

Non-communicable (noninfectious) diseases or illnesses are those that cannot be transmitted from an infected person to a susceptible, healthy one.

Delineating the causes of noncommunicable diseases is often more difficult because several, or even many, factors may contribute to the development of a given non-communicable health condition. These contributing factors may be genetic, environmental, or behavioral in nature. For this reason, many non-communicable health conditions are called multicausation diseases; an example of such is heart disease. Genetics, environmental factors such as stress, and behavioral choices such as poor diet and lack of exercise can all contribute to heart disease.

Acute and Chronic Diseases or Illnesses

In the acute/chronic classification scheme, diseases are classified by their duration of symptoms.

Acute diseases, are diseases in which the peak severity of symptoms occurs and subsides within three months (usually sooner) and the recovery of those who survive is usually complete. Examples of acute communicable diseases include the common cold, influenza (flu), chickenpox, measles, mumps, Rocky Mountain spotted fever, and plague. Examples of acute noncommunicable illnesses are appendicitis, injuries from motor vehicle crashes, acute alcohol intoxication or drug overdose, and sprained ankles.

Chronic diseases or conditions are those in which symptoms continue longer than three months, and in some cases, for the remainder of one's life. Recovery is slow and sometimes incomplete. These diseases can be either communicable or non-communicable. Examples of chronic communicable diseases are AIDS, tuberculosis, herpes virus infections, syphilis, and Lyme disease. Chronic non-communicable illnesses include hypertension, hypercholesterolemia, coronary heart disease, diabetes, and many types of arthritis and cancer.

Communicable Diseases

While infectivity refers to the ability of a biological agent to lodge and grow in a host, the term pathogenicity refers to an infectious disease agent's ability to produce disease. Under certain conditions, pathogenic, biological agents can be transmitted from an infected individual in the community to an uninfected, susceptible one. Noncommunicable diseases are unable to be transmitted as such. Communicable disease agents may be further classified, as will be explained later, according to the manner in which they are transmitted. The elements of a simplified communicable disease model—agent, host, and environment. These three factors seem to sum up the minimal requirements for the occurrence and spread of communicable diseases in a population. In this model, the agent is the element that must be present in order for the disease to occur. For example, the influenza virus must be present for a person to become ill with influenza (flu). The host is any susceptible organism—a single-celled organism, a plant, an animal, or a human—invaded by an infectious agent. The environment includes all other factors— physical, biological, or social—that inhibit or promote disease transmission. Communicable disease transmission occurs when a susceptible host and a pathogenic agent exist in an environment conducive to disease transmission.

Chain of Infection

Communicable disease transmission is a complicated but well-studied process that is best understood through a conceptual model known as the chain of infection. Using the chain of infection model, one can visualize the step-by-step process by which communicable diseases spread from an infected person to an uninfected person in the community. The pathogenic (disease-producing) agent leaves its reservoir (infected host) via a portal of exit.

Transmission occurs in either a direct or indirect manner, and the pathogenic agent enters a susceptible host through a portal of entry in order to establish the disease. For example, let us follow the common cold through the chain of infection. The agent (the cold virus) leaves its reservoir (the throat of an infected person), perhaps when the host sneezes. The portals of exit are the nose and mouth. Transmission may be direct if saliva droplets enter the respiratory tract of a susceptible host at close range, or it may be indirect if droplets dry and become airborne. The portal of entry could be the nose or mouth of a susceptible host. The agent enters, and a new infection is established. There are many variations in the chain of infection, depending upon the disease agent, environmental conditions, infectivity, and host susceptibility. For example, the reservoir for a disease may be a case—a person who has the disease—or a carrier—one who is well but infected and is capable of serving as a source of infection.

A (disease) carrier could be one who is incubating the disease, such as a person who is HIV positive but has no signs of AIDS, or one who has recovered from the disease (is asymptomatic), as is sometimes the case in typhoid fever. For some diseases, the reservoir is not humans but animals. ***Diseases for which the reservoir resides in animal populations are called zoonoses.*** Plague, rabies, Rocky Mountain spotted fever, and Lyme disease is zoonoses. **Diseases for which humans are the only known reservoir, like measles, are known as anthroponoses.** Portals of exit and entry vary from disease to disease. Natural portals of exit and examples of diseases that use them are the respiratory tract (colds, influenza, measles, tuberculosis, and whooping cough), urogenital tract (gonorrhea, syphilis, herpes, and AIDS), digestive tract (amoebic dysentery, shigellosis, polio, typhoid fever, and cholera), and skin (ringworm and jock itch).

The skin is actually a good barrier to infection, but it can be bypassed by a hypodermic needle or when there is an open wound. Blood-sucking insects and ticks make their own portals of entry with mouth parts that penetrate the skin. Finally, many pathogenic agents can cross the placenta from mother to fetus (for example, rubella virus, syphilis spirochetes, and hepatitis B virus).

Modes of Transmission

As noted in the previous paragraphs, communicable disease transmission may be direct or indirect.

Direct transmission

Direct transmission implies the immediate transfer of the disease agent between the infected and the susceptible individuals by direct contact "such as touching, biting, kissing, sexual intercourse, or by direct projection (droplet spread) of droplet spray onto the conjunctiva or onto the mucous membranes of the eye, nose or mouth during sneezing, coughing, spitting, singing or talking (usually limited to a distance of one meter or less)." Examples of diseases for which transmission is usually direct are AIDS, syphilis, gonorrhea, rabies, and the common cold.

Indirect transmission

Indirect transmission may be one of three types—airborne, vehicle-borne, or vector-borne.

Airborne transmission

Airborne transmission is the dissemination of microbial aerosols to a suitable portal of entry, usually the respiratory tract. Microbial aerosols are suspensions of dust or droplet nuclei made up wholly or in part of microorganisms. These particles may remain suspended and infective for long periods of time. Tuberculosis, influenza, histoplasmosis, and legionellosis are examples of airborne diseases.

Vehicle-borne transmission

In vehicle-borne transmission, contaminated materials or objects (fomites) serve as vehicles—nonliving objects by which communicable agents are transferred to a susceptible host. The agent may or may not have multiplied or developed on the vehicle. Examples of vehicles include toys, handkerchiefs, soiled clothes, bedding, food service utensils, and surgical instruments. Also considered vehicles are water, milk, food, or biological products such as blood, serum, plasma, organs, and tissues. Almost any disease can be transmitted by vehicles, including those for which the primary mode of transmission is direct, such as dysentery and hepatitis.

Vectorborne transmission

Vectorborne transmission is the transfer of disease by a living organism such as a mosquito, fly, or tick. Transmission may be mechanical, via the contaminated mouth parts or feet of the vector, or biological, which involves multiplication or developmental changes of the agent in the vector before transmission occurs. In mechanical transmission, multiplication and development of the disease organism usually do not occur. For example, organisms that cause dysentery, polio, cholera, and typhoid fever have been isolated from insects such as cockroaches and houseflies and could presumably be deposited on food prepared for human consumption.

Biological transmission

In biological transmission, multiplication and/or developmental changes of the disease agent occur in the vector before transmission occurs. Biological transmission is much more important than mechanical transmission in terms of its impact on community health. Examples of biological vectors include mosquitoes, fleas, lice, ticks, flies, and other insects. Mosquitoes are by far the most important vectors of human disease. They transmit the viruses that cause yellow fever and dengue fever as well as more than 200 other viruses, including West Nile fever virus. They also transmit malaria, which infects 100 million people in the world each year (mostly in tropical areas), killing at least a million of them. Ticks, another important vector, transmit Rocky Mountain spotted fever, relapsing fever, and Lyme disease. Other insect vectors (and the diseases they transmit) are flies (African sleeping sickness, onchocerciasis, loiasis, and leishmaniasis), fleas (plague and murine typhus), lice (epidemic typhus and trench fever), and kissing bugs (Chagas' disease).

Non-communicable Diseases

While communicable diseases remain an important concern for communities, certain non-communicable diseases, such as heart disease, stroke, and cancer, now rank high among the nation's leading causes of death. While these diseases are not infectious, they nonetheless can occur in epidemic proportions. Furthermore, the chronic nature of many of these diseases means that they can deplete a community's resources quite rapidly. The complex etiologies (causes) of many non-communicable diseases, such as coronary heart disease, are best illustrated by the multicausation disease model. In this model, the human host is pictured in the center of the environment in which he or she lives. Within the host, there exists a unique genetic endowment that is inalterable. The host exists in an environment comprising a multitude of factors that can contribute to the disease process. These environmental factors may be physical, chemical, biological, or social in nature. Physical factors include the latitude, climate, and physical geography of where one lives. The major health risks in the tropics—communicable and parasitic diseases—are different

from those in temperate regions with cold winters—difficulty in finding food and remaining warm. Chemical factors include not only natural chemical hazards of polluted water and air but also the added pollutants of our modern, industrial society. Biological hazards include communicable disease agents such as pathogenic viruses, bacteria, and fungi. Social factors include one's choice of occupation, recreational activities, and living arrangements. Poor choices in life can increase one's risk factors, which is detrimental to one's health.

Heart and related diseases

The disease of the heart and other heart-related diseases, cardiovascular diseases (CVDs), is a leading cause of death in developing to developed countries. In 2020, more than seventy thousand people died of heart disease in the United States and it was estimated that more than 64 million Americans have one or more types of CVD. The American Heart Association lists nine types of CVDs: CHD, stroke, high blood pressure, arrhythmias, diseases of the arteries, congestive heart failure, valvular heart disease, rheumatic fever/rheumatic heart disease, and congenital heart defects. CHD causes more than half of all cardiovascular disease deaths. Sometimes called coronary artery disease, CHD is characterized by damage to the coronary arteries, the blood vessels that carry oxygen-rich blood to the heart muscle. Damage to the coronary arteries usually evolves from the condition known as atherosclerosis, a narrowing of the blood vessels. This narrowing usually results from the build-up of fatty deposits on the inner walls of arteries. When blood flow to the heart muscle is severely reduced or interrupted, a heart attack can occur. If heart damage is severe, the heart may stop beating—a condition known as cardiac arrest.

Over the half of the century, a more complete understanding of the processes involved in CVDs has resulted in a 56% decline in deaths from heart disease and stroke. Numerous risk factors—factors that increase the likelihood of experiencing coronary artery disease—have been identified. While some of these factors cannot be altered by changes in lifestyle or behavior, others can. Factors that cannot be altered include one's age, sex, race, and the genetic tendency toward developing the disease. Factors that can be modified include cigarette smoking, high blood pressure, high blood cholesterol, physical inactivity, obesity, diabetes, and stress.

Cerebrovascular disease (stroke) is the third leading cause of death in developing nations. During a stroke or cerebrovascular accident, the blood supply to the brain is interrupted. The risk factors for developing cerebrovascular disease are similar to those for CHD and include hereditary, behavioral, and environmental factors. Hypertension and cigarette smoking are especially important risk factors for cerebrovascular disease.

Cancer

More than billions of people died from malignant neoplasms (cancer) in the last ten years making it the second leading cause of death all over the world. Malignant neoplasms occur when cells lose control over their growth and division. Normal cells are inhibited from continual growth and division by virtue of their contact with adjacent cells. Malignant (cancerous) cells are not so inhibited; they continue to grow and divide, eventually piling up in a "new growth," a neoplasm or tumor. Early-stage tumors or in situ cancers are more treatable than later-stage cancers. As tumor growth continues, parts of the neoplasm can break off and be carried to distant parts of the body, where they can lodge and continue to grow. When this occurs, the cancer is said to have metastasized. When malignant neoplasms have spread to distant parts of the body and have established new tumors, the cancer is said to be invasive. The more the malignancy spreads, the more difficult it is to treat and the lower the survival rates.

Cancer sites with the highest number of reported cases are the prostate gland (men) and breast (women), but cancer frequently occurs in other sites, including the lung, colon and rectum, pancreas, uterus, ovaries, mouth, bladder, and skin. Lung cancer is the leading cause of cancer deaths in both sexes. There were an estimated more than 10 million cases of lung cancer and an estimated a million lung cancer deaths in 2018 alone. It has been estimated that 87% of these deaths can be attributed to smoking. Alcohol and smokeless tobacco contribute to cancers of the mouth, throat, larynx, esophagus, and liver.

Approximately one million new cases of basal cell or squamous cell skin cancer are detected each year. Almost all of these cases are attributable to exposure to UV-2 radiation from the sun, and yet many people continue to sunbathe or use tanning salons, believing that a tanned body is a healthy one. The number of cases of nonmelanoma skin cancer is expected to rise as long as the ozone layer in the atmosphere continues to be eroded. This is an example of how environmental policy impacts public health.

Other non-communicable diseases

Other non-communicable diseases of major concern are (1) chronic obstructive pulmonary disease and allied conditions, (2) diabetes mellitus, and (3) chronic liver disease and cirrhosis. Each of these chronic non-communicable diseases is a burden not only on the afflicted individuals and their families but on the community's health resources as well.

XIII

EPIDEMIOLOGY: POPULATION GENETICS

Overview

Genetics has come to play an increasingly important role in studies of health and disease driven both by new technologies that enable these studies (chromosome analysis, DNA sequencing, and genotyping) and by our recognition of the key role of genes and genetic variation in disease causation. Humans have 23 pairs of chromosomes made up of some 3 billion nucleotides (A, C, G, and T) of DNA. There are over 20,000 genes scattered across the human chromosomes, most containing in their DNA sequences the information for the amino acid sequence and time/place of expression of a particular protein. We receive one chromosome (and one copy of each of the genes on that chromosome) from our mother and one from our father. Variation in the DNA sequence can result in different alleles or forms of the gene and these individual differences are inherited according to Mendel's laws of transmission resulting in dominant, recessive, or X-linked forms of inheritance. This variation in the DNA sequence is found about once in every 1,000 nucleotides and as of this writing more than 5 million of these variants are well characterized.

The variation occurs in two common forms. The most common and studied are SNPs or single nucleotide polymorphisms – changes in a single DNA nucleotide at a single position (A for G, for example) that are easy to characterize and enumerate. Since we have two copies of each chromosome, one from each parent (and each gene on those chromosomes), we can define a genotype as the type of each of the two possible variants we might have (AA, AG, or GG for an A/G containing SNP). Technology allows the assay of anywhere from one to one million of these per person very cost effectively. The second common form of variation is CNVs or copy number variants where long segments of DNA may be present in zero to many copies. When these segments include genes they can result in the absence of a gene product (if both parents contribute zero copies) to a many-fold increase above the average amount of gene product if multiple gene copies are present. CNVs, while clearly of great biological importance, present more challenges in analysis and are less well characterized than SNPs as of this writing and so we will use SNPs in most examples to follow.

Families share not only environmental factors (including social factors), but also genetic factors. Epidemiologists have traditionally looked for environmental causes for variations in health outcomes, while geneticists have focused on genetic factors of importance for health.

The Occurrence of Genetic Diseases

A genetic disease can be used to describe a broad range of disorders from those caused by chromosome abnormalities or single-gene disruptions to complex multifactorial conditions resulting from the interplay of multiple genes and environmental factors. Single-gene disorders have a long history in public health and genetic epidemiology. Phenylketonuria (PKU) was described by ***Ivar Asbjørn Følling*** in the 1930s as a recessive biochemical disorder of amino acid metabolism that, untreated, leads to profound mental retardation. ***Robert Guthrie*** developed a cheap and efficient test for PKU that, coupled with the recognition that an early dietary limitation of phenylalanine in the diet could prevent the disease manifestations, led to the first effective population-based newborn screening tests. The PKU model is now widely applied throughout the developed world for a wide range of biochemical disorders as well as hypothyroidism and haemoglobinopathies. One haemoglobin disorder, sickle cell anaemia, was first described as a molecular disease by ***Linus Pauling*** in 1949, and in the 1950s it was recognized that carriers for this autosomal recessive disease were resistant to falciparum Malaria while the affected homozygotes had high mortality in early childhood. A third common recessive disorder, cystic fibrosis (CF) was one of the first human disorders to have its gene identified using genome mapping technologies, and the evolution of these technologies is now enabling the application of genetic testing as one additional method available to the epidemiologist and clinician in evaluating the role of genetic factors in disease aetiology.

Another public health success has been the near elimination of the health consequences of Rhesus blood group (Rh) incompatibility between mother and foetus. An Rh+ foetus carried by an Rh– mother can induce an antibody response which results in the destruction of foetal red blood cells and subsequent anaemia which, when severe, can result in death. Recognition of this genetic incompatibility led to prenatal screening and treatment of affected infants as well as effective prevention through the use of antiglobulins given to the mother during and following pregnancy to prevent the induction of the antibody response which would be exacerbated in future pregnancies. Prenatal testing also achieved prominence on a population scale when amniocentesis allowed collection of foetal cells for evaluation of chromosome anomalies such as Trisomy 21 (Down's syndrome). Currently such prenatal screening also includes ultrasound evaluation of foetal organs and maternal serum testing to determine risks for chromosomal aneuploidy and neural tube defects. In the aggregate these testing options allow a better descriptive epidemiology and introduced new screening tools. Single-gene and chromosomal disorders are now easy to define and describe with high degrees of reliability.

They are not limited to the paediatric age groups. Adult onset disorders such as the autosomal dominant cardiomyopathies or long QT syndrome have also been defined and testing has been made available. Current major challenges are now focused on those more common yet complex disorders that have an underlying genetic component but where cause may involve multiple genes as well as environmental triggers that make the identification of specific risk components difficult. Disorders such as type 2 diabetes, inflammatory bowel disease, cardiovascular disease, obesity, dementia, and others are all common, yet complex, making genetic risk factor identification both more compelling and more challenging.

The role of the apolipo protein E (ApoE) gene, and in particular the E4 allele, in predisposing to Alzheimer's disease, was until a few years ago one of the few successful factor identifications to date for a common disease of adult onset. But recent successes in finding genetic risk factors for age-related macular degeneration, type 2 diabetes, breast cancer, and myocardial infarction suggest that genomic tools enable elucidation of population-based genetic risk factors. It is critical for the student to be aware of the ongoing developments in these areas in order to be able to provide more effective care to patients and also to facilitate involvement of patients in appropriate studies aimed at increasing knowledge and improving treatment. It is an area with a rapid development of technology that stretches statistical techniques to their limit.

Common diseases can also arise as part of the expression of single-gene Mendelian conditions or as a complex trait as defined above. The clinician or public health specialist needs to acknowledge the differences in mechanisms and implications for families as well as population planning. If stroke, myocardial infarction, hypertension, cancer, or diabetes, for example, arise as part of a dominant disorder their frequency may be much higher in an extended family than would be predicted by the prevalence of that disorder.

This uneven distribution will have implications for pre-symptomatic screening in an at-risk family and for recognizing it as a source of etiologic heterogeneity which will need to be incorporated into public health planning. In developed countries most deaths are due to cardiovascular diseases and cancer (about one half of all deaths from these two) with accidents, diabetes, Alzheimer's, and suicide making up other significant categories. Each of these, excepting accidents, have well-recognized genetic components whose categorization and understanding will contribute to designing better methods of prevention and treatment.

The Heritability

Twin and adoption studies suggest that a wide variety of phenotypes have a genetic component to their aetiology. Note that heritability estimates are time and population specific, i.e., the overall influence of genetic factors depends on the amount of environmental variance in the study population and vice versa. If, for example, more equal access to favourable living conditions and health care is introduced in a population, this is likely to decrease the environmental variance and hence increase the proportion of the total variation attributable to genetic factors (the heritability).

On the other hand, an increase in the environmental variance as seen in modern societies can also provide the opportunity for genetic effects to become expressed. A substantial heritability for a trait suggests that it may be possible to identify specific genetic variants that influence the trait. The chance of identifying gene variants affecting a trait through genetic association or family studies depends on the number of gene variants and the size of their effect.

Adoption Studies

For logistic reasons, adoption studies are fewer and usually smaller than other family studies. Nevertheless, adoption studies have had a substantial impact on the nature–nurture debate for a number of traits because these studies have produced remarkable results. Adoption studies use the fact that adoptees share genetic variants with their biological parents but not the parents' environment, and they share the environment to some extent, but not gene variants, with their adoptive families.

Among the most notable findings from adoption studies is **Heston's 1966 study**, where he showed that among 47 children who had schizophrenic mothers and who were put up for adoption 5 developed schizophrenia, while none of the 50 control adoptees developed schizophrenia. Although the sample size is small, the study very convincingly indicated that schizophrenia has a strong genetic component.

A strong intrauterine component could also be an explanation but twin studies reveal much higher concordance rates in monozygotic twins compared to dizygotic twins (see below), again suggesting genetic factors as the major factor in susceptibility to schizophrenia. Another intriguing finding that surprised many was a Danish adoption study of BMI. This study showed that the BMI of adoptees correlated more with the BMI of their biological relatives than that of their adoptive relatives, indicating a strong genetic or early life component to variation in body composition in settings with no shortage of food supply.

Twin Studies

In humans two types of twinning occur: monozygotic (identical) twins, who share all their genetic material, and dizygotic (fraternal) twins, who on average share 50% of their genes by descent like non-twin siblings. A twin study of a condition/disease in its simplest form is based on a comparison of monozygotic and dizygotic concordance rates. A significantly higher concordance rate in monozygotic than in dizygotic twins indicates that genetic factors play a role in the aetiology of the disease. For continuous traits, correlations are used instead of concordance rates. The twin study does not identify specific genes that affect the trait but rather assesses the overall effect of genetic factors: the degree to which differences in the phenotype are attributable to genetic differences between people. To estimate the heritability of a trait (i.e., the proportion of the population variance attributable to genetic variation) twin data can be analysed using standard biometric models.

A number of recent developments in twin methodology have taken place based on the incorporation of genotypes. This enables twin models to estimate how much of the genetic variation is due to variation in a specific gene. The classic twin methodology is based on genetic theory and the fundamental idea is that a higher degree of similarity for a trait within monozygotic twins compared to dizygotic twins is attributable to the higher degree of genetic similarity in monozygotic twins.

Twin studies of Alzheimer's disease (not early onset) show that a co-twin of an affected monozygotic twin has a 60–80% risk of becoming affected, while the risk is 30–40% if the pair is dizygotic. For Parkinson's disease the corresponding numbers are about 5% for both monozygotic and dizygotic twins. This is compatible with a strong genetic influence on Alzheimer's disease while most etiological factors for Parkinson's disease are likely to be identified in the environment some genetic risks for Parkinson's disease are now known. Twin studies are not theoretical models such as the component causal model. Under such models it is easy to argue that all diseases are 100% genetically and 100% environmentally determined because it is hard to imagine any disease that does not have both environmental and genetic components.

However, in the practical research process of identifying factors influencing disease occurrence in a given setting at a given time the classic twin study is very useful. Twin studies can point toward identifiable causes of variation in a given population, e.g., to which degree it is likely that genetic differences between people play a major role for the occurrence of that disease in that population, as seen in the Alzheimer's disease occurrence described above.

Half-Sib Studies

In countries with population registers it is possible, on a nationwide level, to identify individuals who have changed their spouse or residence (or other environmental factors). Information from these registers can be used to set up a study that is particularly well suited for studying nature–nurture effects on reproductive outcomes or diseases in early childhood.

Gene-Environment Interaction

It is difficult to imagine diseases that are not at least in part due to interactions between genetic and environmental factors. A clear example of gene–environment interaction is G6PD deficiency. This is an X-linked trait of the enzyme glucose-6- phosphate dehydrogenase deficiency that facilitates energy metabolism in cells (like red blood cells) and helps protect the cell from oxidative damage. Defects in the enzyme that are genetically determined are extremely common (~5% worldwide) and can result in haemolysis and anaemia if the affected are exposed to certain nutritional insults such as Fava beans or pharmacologic agents including some antibiotics and anti-malarials. Thus individuals with a risk genotype are normal in the absence of an environmental exposure. This is an example where the causal field model fits the observation.

The strength between the genetic factor and the disease depends upon the prevalence of the dietary factors and medicine use. By avoiding these environmental exposures we make sure the causal field is not completed. Also the common ApoE-4 polymorphism, which has been shown to be a risk factor for cardiovascular diseases and Alzheimer's disease, seems to be involved in gene–environment interaction making the ApoE-4 carrier more susceptible to environmental exposures. For example, an increased risk of chronic brain injury after head trauma has been observed for individuals who carry the ApoE-4 gene variant, compared to non-ApoE-4 carriers.

A huge challenge to gene–environment interaction studies is the multiple comparison problem. With approximately 20,000 genes already identified, many having several variants, an enormous number of possible gene–environment interactions can be studied. One reasonable strategy is testing of biologically plausible interactions and replication of positive findings in large studies.

Cross-Sectional Studies of Genetic Polymorphisms

If we did not already know from vital statistics that males have substantially higher mortality than females throughout life, we could get information about this from a cross-sectional population-based study. We would see that in many countries the distribution of males to females would be approximately 1:1 at birth while it is about 1:2 at age 85 and 1:4 or even 1:5 at age 100 in many settings. Similarly some genetic variants, e.g., ApoE-4, are "weeded out" with age, indicating that they are associated with increased mortality. Interference from such cross-sectional studies is dependent on a stable population with little migration into the population. Remote islands will therefore often be very well suited for such cross-sectional age-dependency studies while immigrant countries like the USA and Australia are less suited.

Incorporation of Genetic Variables in Epidemiologic Studies

Advances in technology frequently enable new and more powerful analytic approaches to disease causality. While it has been possible to include variability in genes into studies of epidemiology since the discovery of the human blood group antigens in the early 1900s, there has been a remarkable advance in using genetic variables in the last few years as DNA sequencing and related technologies make it feasible to study up to 1 million variants per individual on thousands of cases and controls at practical costs.

Two general options are currently available for large epidemiologic studies. One is directly hypothesis driven and involves choosing a modest number of variants for study when the underlying biology/physiology of the risk alleles is already known or highly suspected. This is called the candidate gene approach and might be used in a setting of building on a known effect such as the role of ApoE variants in dementia or cardiovascular disease or genes such as the N-acetyltransferases that are critical in cigarette smoke detoxification.

Selecting for study variants in genes of known biological function enables the investigator to add a powerful new variable to the analysis and limits the problems that arise from multiple comparisons and the attendant issue of false positive results (type 1 errors). If we has no strong candidates or wishes to investigate the role of common variants without a prior hypothesis as to what genes those variants might be present in one can use the genome wide association study (GWAS).

In 2007 advances in both technology for variant detection (a range of "DNA chips") and analytic advances in how to address the type 1 error problem resulted in an explosion of GWAS studies leading to the identification possible of gene variants contributing to a wide range of common, complex disorders. The technology allows the study of up to 1 million single nucleotide polymorphisms (SNPs) as well as 1 million copy number variants (CNVs) on a single individual for less than 500 Euros. This technology takes advantage of the observation that common human genetic variation is located in blocks where tens or even hundreds of variants in physical proximity on a chromosome each have their individual alleles inherited in a manner highly correlated with the alleles of nearby SNPs. Thus any one SNP can serve as a surrogate marker for many others, making it practical to provide coverage of an entire genome with a few hundred thousand SNPs and CNVs. As the cost of the assays is expected to drop further such approaches are now a standard tool in genetic epidemiologic studies.

There are a few caveats. First, the approach is only effective when common variants contributing to disease can be detected by virtue of their disease association. While this is true for some single-gene disorders (cystic fibrosis, for example) as well as complex traits (breast cancer and many others) it is not true for all disorders (PKU and hypertension seem to be exceptions). In these disorders, a genetic component may still be very active but a large number of different alleles may be contributing so that no common variant can be detected by association. These multiple allele disorders can be solved by DNA sequencing, and while the cost of DNA sequencing is low it remains costly enough that it is not yet in routine use for epidemiologic studies that lack a hypothesis for a specific region to examine.

Next, because of the enormity of the multiple comparisons of there are many signals that may require evaluation so that replication in independent populations for positive results is now an expectation for any such study to be accepted. Nonetheless, GWAS studies are now a component of most large epidemiologic efforts, and plans for obtaining material for DNA should be a standard plan for any study in which a genetic variation might be active.

XIV

EPIDEMIOLOGY: NUTRITION

Introduction

Nutritional epidemiology studies the role of food and nutrition and in relation to disease in human populations. Nutritional epidemiological research involves the role of food and nutrition in aetiology of diseases, assess and monitor the food consumption and nutritional status of populations, measures to prevent, control and improvement of health, develop interventions in order to maintain healthy eating lifestyle and also to analyze the association of nutrition and physical activity in relation to diseases.

Nutritional epidemiology examines the association of diet and our health. Earliest epidemiological investigation dates back to more 2000 years ago, when Hippocrates conducted a clinical trial to observe the cause of a disease and belief in notion that health depends on magical influence. Lind in 1753 observed that scurvy was caused by deficiency of vitamin C when he conducted one of the earliest clinical trials with lemons and oranges. Milestones in classic epidemiology. Casimir Funk in 1912 investigated that deficiency of substances which he called "vitamins" may cause diseases such as sprue, beriberi, rickets, pellagra etc. Another epidemiological investigation of 19th and 20th century include Joseph Goldberger who observed the occurrence of pellagra among poor relying on as staple diet.

He suspected the disease could be due to nutritional deficiency. It was later identified as deficiency of niacin, a B-complex vitamin (B3).

With the discovery of microorganisms, at the end of the 19th century mark the era of infectious disease epidemiology. Robert Edward Koch work on the aetiology of tubercle bacillus in 1882 resulted in improved environmental conditions and interventions for preventing transmission of certain microorganisms. Epidemiological observation thus has provided the insight into the diet disease relationship and the cause and prevention of diseases. Earlier epidemiologist focused on the aetiology of infectious diseases but since early decades of 20th century, they shifted to chronic disease and remarkable contribution have made to the understanding of nutrition-related diseases as well.

Band and Dyerberg considered coronary disease in Eskimos and observed that it was uncommon despite their high fat diet and later found that omega -3 fatty acid from fish oil is responsible for low plasma lipid level in their diet. Hospital based case control study in 1950 showed that smoking was associated with lung cancer. So, epidemiology play an increasingly important role and its evolution has led to the development of specialized areas like environmental, clinical, psychiatric, genetic, occupational within the epidemiology.

Malnutrition

Malnutrition is a condition resulting from faulty nutrition either due to deficiency or excess of one or more essential nutrients or to a failure of the body to digest or absorb the food from the alimentary tract. It can be classified into three categories from nutritional stand point i.e. under-nutrition, over nutrition and micro-nutrient malnutrition.

Macronutrient deficiency (under-nutrition)

Under-nutrition occurs due to inadequate calorie intake or due to non-availability of nutrients due to frequent infections, other metabolic issues or endocrine disturbances.

Protein energy malnutrition (PEM)

Protein-energy malnutrition is often used as a synonym of malnutrition and under-nutrition. The most important factor resulting in PEM are inadequate diet and infectious diseases affecting all segments of the population particularly from the backward and downtrodden communities who do not have proper access to food. PEM covers a wide spectrum of conditions from growth retardation to over kwashiorkor and marasmus.

Kwashiorkor

Diet predominantly deficient in protein often leads to kwashiorkor. Although it occurs in older children and adults, it usually affects children aged 1- 4 years when they are weaned from breast milk to adult diet. Clinical features of kwashiorkor are growth failure, oedema and mental changes. The main sign is oedema usually appears first on the feet and leg and eventually spread to hands and faces. Other symptoms include skin lesions and hypo-pigmentation and in severe cases the epithelium peels off leaving behind de-pigmented patches. The hair shows changes in texture and curly hair becomes straight easily pluckable. Diarrhoea may occur due to secondary infections and defective digestion.

Marasmus

A diet deficient in calories and prolonged starvation results in marasmus. It may also occur due to chronic infections with marginal food intake. It is more common in children below 2 years of age. Main cardinal features include severe muscle wasting, growth retardation and loss of subcutaneous fat. The child appears very thin because most of the muscles mass and fat have been expended to provide energy. Associated vitamin deficiencies are however very common.

Dietary management and prevention

An adequate amount of diet with sufficient calories and a good quality protein should be given. High energy intakes (150kcal/kg) and high protein intakes (3-4g/kg) are required for rapid recovery. During infancy and childhood protein requirement is more. In pregnancy protein requirement is increased by another 15-20 gram per day. Liquid diet either fresh milk or dry skimmed milk powder is recommended. Eggs are desirable as sources of protein. Vitamins and mineral supplements are recommended for all malnourished children. Besides, dietary management it is also necessary for health promotion at community and household level. Promotion of breast feeding, measure to improve family diet, distribution of supplements, routine immunization of children, and periodic surveillance of child's diet should be encouraged. In India, the Integrated Child Development Services (ICDS) is a major national program providing integrated health and nutrition services to preschool children.

Micro-nutrient malnutrition

It refers to a group of conditions caused by deficiencies of essential minerals and vitamins. The most common types of micro-nutrient malnutrition in India and in most developing countries include:

Iron Deficiency Anaemia (IDA): Nutritional anaemia is a major public health problem affecting all sections of the society. It is defined by WHO as a condition in which the haemoglobin content is low as a result of deficiency of one or more essential nutrients, regardless of the cause of deficiency. The major cause of nutritional anaemia is due to deficiency of iron, vitamin B12 and vitamin C. Burden of anaemia are not only confined to pregnant women but affects other segments of the society. Adolescent boys and girls, women in reproductive years, infants and young children and pregnant women are in vulnerable groups Prevalence of anaemia in India is high due to low dietary intake, poor iron and folic acid intake, poor bio-availability of iron in phytate fibre-rich Indian diet. NFHS- 3 reported prevalence of anaemia as 55 % in women aged 15–49 years, 24% in men aged 15–49 years and 70% among children aged 6–59 months. Deficiency of iron increases incidence of maternal deaths by 20% increases the risk of premature delivery and low birth weight. According to WHO, 12.8% maternal mortality in Asia are attributed to anaemia. Iron rich supplements are a must for prevention of anaemia. Oral iron or low dosage of iron, multivitamin supplements, folic acid, vitamin A and zinc are recommended.

Vitamin A Deficiency (VAD): Vitamin A deficiency with a variety of manifestations is wide spread in the world today. Deficiency of vitamin A leading to xerophthalmia and night blindness among young children has become a major public health problem in developing countries including India. The term xerophthalmia comprehensively includes all ocular manifestations of vitamin A deficiency. The most contributing factor is due to inadequate of vitamin A or its precursor i.e. β carotene. The most vulnerable groups are the pregnant women and infants born particularly in low income groups.

According to the estimates of NFHS 2, the prevalence of night blindness due to low dietary intake of vitamin A in pregnant women was up to 10-20%. Vitamin `deficiency predominantly occurs in children due to common childhood infections like diarrhoea, measles, and infestations like giardiasis and ascariasis. Micronutrient Initiative (MI) estimates that around 3, 30,000 children in India die due to VAD. More than 4 million children worldwide exhibit signs of severe deficiency.

Thiamine (Vitamin B1) Deficiency Disorders

Deficiency of thiamine causes beriberi and the severity is determined by the degree and duration of deficiency. Cardiac beriberi or wet beriberi is characterized by biventricular heart failure, peripheral vasoconstriction, wide pulse pressure and oedema. An acute form documented as pernicious beriberi is characterized by sudden onset of cardiac pain, restlessness, and peripheral circulatory failure. Atrophic or dry beriberi is often prevalent in India and its symptoms include numbness, loss of function or paralysis of lower extremities due to multiple neuritis. Both the type of beriberi show muscle degeneration, loss of motor function and loss of sensation.

Aetiology of water soluble vitamin deficiencies includes inadequate due to poverty, faulty cooking habits, losses due to storage, impaired absorption due to chronic diarrhoea, metabolic functions such as genetic abnormalities, metabolic stress. Adequate food source of thiamine are sufficient to prevent any of the deficiency. Parboiled rice and un-milled rice are an excellent source of thiamine and hence should be encouraged. The most appropriate approach to meet the nutritional needs is to encourage consumption of inexpensive and locally available foods and to educate the public to improve the dietary and cooking habits.

Riboflavin (vitamin B12) Deficiency Disorders

The deficiency of riboflavin is widely prevalent in low income groups of the population in all age groups. Clinical manifestation of riboflavin deficiency includes ocular symptoms with characteristic itching, burning, fatigue and eyestrain. Other symptoms are shiny red mucosa of lips with cracking at the corners of the mouth, known as cheilosis and roughened skin around the mouth and nose. For control and prevention diet rich in riboflavin such as meats, milk, pulses, and other dairy products are recommended.

Iodine Deficiency Disorders (IDD)

Iodine is an essential micro-nutrients and deficiency of which causes a wide variety of neurological and physiological development. The term "Iodine Deficiency Disorders" was introduced by Hetzel, 1987. The major clinical manifestation of iodine deficiency is goiter, defined by non-inflammatory enlargement of thyroid gland. For clinical assessments, goiter size is assessed based on the palpation of thyroid and classified as follows:

i. Grade 0- No goiter (if it is not visible or palpable if palpable but the size is less than the distal phalange).
v. Grade I- Not visible when the neck is in normal position, but palpable (the size of the enlargement of gland should be more than the size of the distal phalange of the thumb of the subject).
v. Grade III- Visible from the minimum distance.

Environmental factors such as environmental iodine deficiency and goitrogens (substances which interfere with the metabolism of iodine in the body) leads to endemic IDD while intrinsic factors like hormonal imbalance, failure to synthesis the thyroid hormone contributes to sporadic cases. Iodine deficiency disorders include a spectrum of disorders such as goiter, retarded physical development, impaired mental function, juvenile hypothyroidism in children and adolescents, psychomotor defects, congenital anomalies in foetus.

Nutrition and Non-Communicable Diseases (NCDs)

Massive economic development, rapid urbanization, food security and increase health care services in developing countries there has been decline in under nutrition-related diseases. However, these factors on the other hand have exacerbated the development of chronic diseases, also known as non-communicable diseases (NCDs) due to unhealthy diets, sedentary lifestyles and lack of physical activity. NCDs are now a major global burden in public health. In has been reported that in 2001, 60% of the 56.5 million global deaths were from chronic diseases, such as cardiovascular diseases, hyperlipidaemia, hypertension, cancer, and diabetes. In both developing and developed countries, due to nutritional transition, unhealthy dietary and lifestyle pattern chronic non communicable diseases have become principal global causes of morbidity and mortality.

Obesity

Obesity defined by excessive accumulation of body fat resulting in adverse effect on health is associated with other chronic diseases. The fundamental cause of obesity is excessive consumption of high calorie foods with less physical activity level i.e. when the energy intake is in excess of expenditure. Though obesity can be determined by many other methods, calculation of BMI defined as weight (in kg) divided by height (in meters square), is widely used to classify underweight, overweight and obesity in adults. It is considered as a practical indicator of the severity of obesity. Obesity has multi-factorial epidemiology such as genetic, environmental, psychological, age, sex and socio-economic factors. The determinant of obesity are urbanization, nutritional transitional, globalization of food production, i.e. the shift towards highly refined foods, meat, dairy products of high level saturated fats have, together with reduced energy expenditure, contributed to rises in the incidence of obesity and non-communicable diseases. Obesity is associated with other diseases such as diabetes, cardiovascular diseases, hypertension, cancers and polycystic ovarian diseases. In India, particularly in urban setting, obesity is emerging as an important health problem. According to NFHS 3 report, 9% of Indian men and 13% of women are overweight or obese. Dietary prevention for obesity include limited intake of fats, elimination of trans fatty acids, increasing physical activity level , reducing intakes drinks high in sugars, limited salt consumption, increase consumption of fruits and vegetables, can prevent unhealthy weight gain.

Type 2 diabetes

Type 2 diabetes often referred to as non-insulin dependent diabetes, mellitus is characterized by insulin resistance where the body is unable to utilize the glucose derived from carbohydrates food or glycogen store in the tissues. Diagnosis of type 2 diabetes usually occurs on the onset of middle adulthood and is associated with obesity which lead to elevated blood sugar and itself can lead to insulin resistance. This type of diabetes is the most common type and nearly 90-95% of all diabetic belongs to this category and is distinguished from type 1 diabetes and gestational diabetes of pregnancy. There is increasing reports of children with type 2 diabetes and have become serious health issues. It has been estimated in the adult population that the prevalence of diabetes mellitus will raise from 4% in 1995 to 5.4% in 2025.

Obesity is a major risk factor for development of non-insulin dependent diabetes. Approximately type 2 diabetic patients are either found to be overweight or obese and impaired glucose tolerance is also common in this group. Many epidemiological research revealed that central obesity as assessed by waist hip ratio (WHR) is associated with a higher occurrence of diabetes. Diet rich in energy dense food such as carbohydrates which contribute to high calorie and enhance body weight have been associated with diabetes. Other risk factors associated with development of type 2 diabetes include physical inactivity, diet, increasing age, insulin resistance, ethnicity, family history of diabetes, and genetic factors.

XV

EPIDEMIOLOGY: DISEASE OUTBREAK

Here, we will discuss the three major types of outbreaks viz. waterborne disease outbreak, foodborne disease outbreak, and vectorborne disease outbreak.

Waterborne Disease Outbreak

Waterborne diseases occur when water, contaminated with a disease agent, is consumed by a susceptible person. Waterborne disease agents include viruses, bacteria, parasites, and chemicals. Waterborne viral agents and the diseases they cause include poliomyelitis virus (polio) and hepatitis A virus (hepatitis). Waterborne bacteria and the diseases they cause include *Escherichia coli*, *Salmonella typhi* (typhoid fever), *Shigella* spp. (shigellosis or bacillary dysentery), and *Vibrio cholerae* (cholera). Waterborne parasites include *Entamoeba histolytica* (amebiasis or amoebic dysentery), Giardia lamblia (giardiasis), and Cryptosporidium parvum (cryptosporidiosis). Each of these diseases can be serious, and two in particular—typhoid fever and cholera—have killed thousands of people in single epidemics.

One of the earliest carefully documented cholera epidemics was the one that occurred in London, England, in 1849. This epidemic occurred before the discoveries of Louis Pasteur, during a period of time when most people thought that diseases were caused by malodorous vapours (miasmas) or, perhaps, by spirits. Dr. John Snow believed that water drawn from a particular city well was contaminated. After interviewing many sick and well people, he had the handle removed from the Broad Street pump; the cholera epidemic subsided. This event was so remarkable that the site has been preserved in modern-day London.

A waterborne disease outbreak (WBDO) is an event in which at least two persons experience a similar illness after ingestion of drinking water or after exposure to water used for recreational purposes and epidemiologic evidence implicates water as the probable source of the illness. In the case of chemical poisoning, a single case is considered an outbreak. WBDOs can be associated with drinking water, recreational water, or occupational water exposure. In recent years, the leading causes of WBDOs (in cases in which the cause was identified) have been bacteria and parasites. During the 1999–2000 reporting period, the cause could only be determined in 56.4% of the outbreaks associated with drinking water. Where cause was determined, bacteria were most often the cause, followed by parasites, viruses, and chemicals. For outbreaks associated with recreational water, the cause was determined 74.6% of the time; the leading cause of WBDOs associated with recreational water was parasites (Cryptosporidium), followed by bacteria (*E. coli* and *Shigell*a), and viruses. One of the most significant achievements in public health during the last century occurred not by removing harmful elements from community drinking water, but by adding something to it.

Foodborne Disease Outbreak

Foodborne Diseases One way in which humans interact with their environment is by ingesting bits of it. The act of eating is, in effect, a way of bringing biological hazards into intimate contact with the tissues that line the intestinal tract. "More than 200 known diseases are transmitted through food. In these cases, food is the vehicle; and the agents can be viruses, bacteria, parasite's toxins, metals, and prions." Symptoms of foodborne illness range from mild to severe, and organs involved can include stomach and intestines, liver, kidneys, and brain and nervous system. Foodborne diseases cause between 6 and 81 million cases of illness and up to 9,000 deaths each year in the United States.6A majority of these cases are never reported to the Centres for Disease Control and Prevention (CDC). The CDC defines a foodborne disease outbreak (FBDO) as the occurrence of two or more cases of a similar illness resulting from the ingestion of food.7 During the five-year period 1993–1997, only 878 (32%) of the 2,751 FBDOs reported to the CDC had a known aetiology. These outbreaks accounted for 50,788 (59%) of the 86,058 infections reported. Among the outbreaks for which the causative agent was established, bacterial pathogens caused 75% of the outbreaks and 86% of the cases. Salmonella serotype enteritis accounted for the largest number of outbreaks, cases, and deaths, but *E. coli* O157:H7 was also responsible for multistate outbreaks that were associated with consumption of under cooked or raw ground beef. One of the food safety objectives of Healthy People 2010 is to reduce outbreaks of infections caused by key foodborne bacteria by half. Chemicals were the cause of 17% of outbreaks (1% of cases) in which the cause was determined, viruses for 6% of outbreaks (8% of cases), and parasites for 2% of outbreaks (5% of cases).

The leading factors that were found to contribute to FBDOs during 1993–1997 were improper holding temperatures and inadequate cooking of food. Other factors that often contribute to FBDOs are poor personal hygiene of preparers, contaminated equipment, and obtaining food from an unsafe source (such as shellfish from polluted waters). Almost any food can serve as a vehicle of transmission for a foodborne disease agent. The vehicle of infection for more than half of the cases is unknown. In some outbreaks, multiple foods are incriminated. Delicatessens, cafeterias, and restaurants are reported nearly twice as often as homes as places where the contaminated food is eaten. Also, more cases occur in the summer months than during any other season. More and more of our foods are imported. Currently, 38% of the fruits, 12% of the vegetables, and 9% of the meats and poultry Americans consume each year are imported. Foodborne illness has been increasingly related to imported foods.

To protect the public from foodborne diseases requires the coordinated efforts of federal, state, and local health agencies. At the federal level, the CDC, under its Emerging Infections Program, has established the Foodborne Diseases Active Surveillance Network (Food Net) to provide better data on foodborne diseases. Food Net tracks nine foodborne diseases in eight catchment areas with a combined surveillance population of 29.5 million people. The CDC coordinates these surveillance activities with officials from the U.S. Department of Agriculture's Food Safety and Inspection Service, the Food and Drug Administration's Centre for Food Safety and Applied Nutrition, and with the respective state epidemiologists.

A recent report analysed the success rate for investigating and reporting FBDOs in Food Net catchment areas during 1998–1999. The results were disappointing. In 71% of the outbreaks, no confirmed aetiology (cause) was found, and in 46% of the outbreaks, no suspected food was identified. This study illustrates the difficulty of epidemiological and disease control work in the absence of adequate resources. Enforcing state regulations at the local level are sanitarians, also known as registered environmental health specialists. Hired by local health departments, these sanitarians inspect restaurants and other food-serving establishments (such as hospitals, nursing homes, churches, and schools), temporary and seasonal points of food service (such as those at fairs and festivals), and retail food outlets (grocery stores and supermarkets) to ensure that environmental conditions favourable to the growth and development of pathogens do not exist. By enforcing food safety laws, public health officials protect the health of the community by reducing the incidence of FBDOs. In fact, safer and healthier foods have been one of the ten greatest achievements in public health in the twentieth century.

Vectorborne Diseases Outbreak

Standing water, including runoff water from overflowing septic systems or overloaded sewer systems, and improperly handled solid waste are more than unsavoury sights. They provide habitat for, and support the proliferation of, disease vectors. A vector is a living organism, usually an insect or other arthropod that transmits microscopic disease agents to susceptible hosts. Examples of vectors and the diseases they transmit include mosquitoes (malaria, filariasis, and arthropodborne viruses—arboviruses), fleas (murine typhus and plague), lice (epidemic typhus), and ticks (Rocky Mountain spotted fever and Lyme disease).

Mosquito larvae require standing water in which to complete their development. The improper handling of wastewater or inadequate drainage of rainwater provides an ideal habitat for mosquitoes and increases the risk for a vectorborne disease outbreak (VBDO). Improper management of solid waste—such as occurs at open dumps, ill-managed landfills, and urban slums—fosters the expansion of rat and mouse populations. These rodents are hosts for fleas, which transmit murine typhus, a rickettsia disease characterized by headache, fever, and rash. If the rodent population should decline rapidly because of disease or a successful rodent control program, these fleas could come into contact with humans and spread the disease directly to them. Diseases of animals that are transmissible to humans, such as murine typhus, are referred to as zoonosis. Seemingly harmless interactions with the environment can have unintended consequences. For example, white-tailed deer were decimated throughout much of the Midwest and the eastern United States during the nineteenth century.

As they declined in numbers, their predators and parasites vanished too. Reintroduced in the 1930s and protected from hunting by strict regulations, white-tailed deer populations became well established. Modern farming practices, which result in field after field of corn, soybeans, or other nutritious crops interspersed with wooded areas, resulted in deer populations large enough to reach pest status in some parts of the Midwest. As deer populations have increased, so have populations of the blacklegged tick, *Ixodes scapularis*. Sometimes called the deer tick, *I. scapularis* is the vector of Lyme disease caused by the bacterial spirochete *Borrelia burgdorferi*. Lyme disease is currently the most commonly reported vectorborne disease in the United States.

XVI

EPIDEMIOLOGY: DISEASE CONTROLE

The aims of epidemiology are to prevent, control, and in rare cases, eradicate diseases.

Prevention implies the planning for and taking of action to prevent or forestall the occurrence of an undesirable event and is, therefore, more desirable than ***intervention***, the taking of action during an event. For example, immunizing to prevent a disease is preferable to taking an antibiotic to cure one.

Control /Controle is a general term for the containment of a disease and can include both prevention and intervention measures. The term control is often used to mean the limiting of transmission of a communicable disease in a population.

Eradication is the uprooting or total elimination of a disease from the human population. It is an elusive goal, one that is only rarely achieved in public health. Smallpox is the only communicable disease that has been eradicated.

Levels of disease prevention

There are three levels of application of preventive measures in disease control—primary, secondary, and tertiary.

The purpose of ***primary prevention*** is to forestall the onset of illness or injury during the prepathogenesis period (before the disease process begins). Examples of primary prevention include health education and health promotion programs, safe-housing projects, and character-building and personality development programs. Other examples are the use of immunizations against specific diseases, the practice of personal hygiene such as hand washing, the use of rubber gloves, and the chlorination of the community's water supply. Unfortunately, disease or injury cannot always be avoided. Chronic diseases in particular sometimes cause considerable disability before they are detected and treated. In these cases, prompt intervention can prevent death or limit disability.

Secondary prevention is the early diagnosis and prompt treatment of diseases before the disease becomes advanced and disability becomes severe. One of the most important secondary prevention measures is health screenings. The aim of these screenings is not to prevent the onset of disease but rather to detect its presence during early pathogenesis, thus permitting early intervention (treatment) and limiting disability. It is important to note that the purpose of a health screening is not to diagnose a disease. Instead, the purpose is to economically and efficiently sort those who are probably healthy from those who could possibly be positive for a disease. Those who screen positively can then be referred for more specific diagnostic procedures. Screenings for diabetes and high blood pressure are popular examples of health screenings, as are breast self-examination and testicular self-examination.

The aim of ***tertiary prevention*** is to retrain, re-educate, and rehabilitate the patient who has already incurred a disability. Tertiary preventive measures include those that are applied after significant pathogenesis has occurred. Therapy for a heart patient is an example of tertiary prevention.

Prevention of Communicable Diseases

Prevention and control efforts for communicable diseases include primary, secondary, and tertiary approaches. Successful application of these approaches, particularly primary prevention, resulting in unprecedented declines in morbidity and mortality from communicable diseases, has been one of the outstanding achievements in public health in this century.

Primary Prevention of Communicable Diseases

The primary prevention measures for communicable diseases can best be visualized using the chain of infection. In this model, prevention strategies are evident at each link in the chain. Successful application of each strategy can be seen as weakening a link, with the ultimate goal of breaking the chain of infection or interrupting the disease transmission cycle. Examples of community measures include chlorination of the water supply, the inspection of restaurants and retail food markets, immunization programs that reach all citizens, the maintenance of a well-functioning sewer system, the proper disposal of solid waste, and the control of vectors and rodents. To these can be added personal efforts at primary prevention, including hand washing, the proper cooking of food, adequate clothing and housing, the use of condoms, and obtaining all the available immunizations against specific diseases.

Secondary Prevention of Communicable Diseases

Secondary preventive measures against communicable diseases for the individual involved

1. self-diagnosis and self-treatment with nonprescription medications or home remedies and
2. diagnosis and treatment with an antibiotic prescribed by a physician.

Secondary preventive measures undertaken by the community against infectious diseases are usually aimed at controlling or limiting the extent of an epidemic. Examples include carefully maintaining records of cases and complying with the regulations requiring the reporting of notifiable diseases and investigating cases and contacts—those who may have become infected through close contact with known cases. Occasionally, secondary disease control measures may include isolation and quarantine. These two practices are quite different from one another and are often confused. Isolation is the separation, for the period of communicability, of infected persons or animals from others so as to prevent the direct or indirect transmission of the communicable agent to a susceptible person. Quarantine is the limitation of the freedom of movement of well persons or animals that have been exposed to a communicable disease until the incubation period has passed. Further control measures may include disinfection, the killing of communicable agents outside of the host, and mass treatment with antibiotics. Finally, public health education and health promotion should be used as both primary and secondary preventive measures.

Tertiary Prevention of Communicable Diseases

Tertiary preventive measures for the control of communicable diseases for the individual include convalescence from infection, recovery to full health, and return to normal activity. In some cases, such as paralytic poliomyelitis, a return to normal activity may not be possible even after extensive physical therapy. At the community level, tertiary preventive measures are aimed at preventing the recurrence of an epidemic. The proper removal, embalming, and burial of the dead is an example. Tertiary prevention may involve the re-application of primary and secondary measures in such a way as to prevent further cases. For example, in the Republic of Korea, people with colds or flu wear gauze masks in public to reduce the spread of disease.

XVII
Bibliography

Gatseva, Penka D.; Argirova, Mariana (1 June 2011). "Public health: the science of promoting health". Journal of Public Health. 19 (3): 205–206. doi:10.1007/s10389-011-0412-8. ISSN 1613-2238. S2CID 1126351.

Winslow, Charles-Edward Amory (1920). "The Untilled Field of Public Health". Modern Medicine. 2 (1306): 183–191. Bibcode:1920Sci....51...23W. doi:10.1126/science.51.1306.23. PMID 17838891.

"What is Public Health". Centers for Disease Control Foundation. Atlanta, GA: Centers for Disease Control. Retrieved 27 January 2017.

What is the WHO definition of health? from the Preamble to the Constitution of WHO as adopted by the International Health Conference, New York, 19 June - 22 July 1946; signed on 22 July 1946 by the representatives of 61 States (Official Records of WHO, no. 2, p. 100) and entered into force on 7 April 1948. The definition has not been amended since 1948.

PERDIGUERO, E. (1 July 2001). "Anthropology in public health. Bridging differences in culture and society". Journal of Epidemiology & Community Health. 55 (7): 528b–528. doi:10.1136/jech.55.7.528b. ISSN 0143-005X. PMC 1731924.

Lincoln C Chen; David Evans; Tim Evans; Ritu Sadana; Barbara Stilwell; Phylida Travis; Wim Van Lerberghe; Pascal Zurn (2006). World Health Report 2006: working together for health. Geneva: WHO. OCLC 71199185.

Jamison, D T; Mosley, W H (January 1991). "Disease control priorities in developing countries: health policy responses to epidemiological change". American Journal of Public Health. 81 (1): 15–22. doi:10.2105/ajph.81.1.15. ISSN 0090-0036. PMC 1404931. PMID 1983911.

Rosen, George (2015). A history of public health (Revised expanded). Baltimore. ISBN 978-1-4214-1601-4. OCLC 878915301.

Porter, Dorothy (1999). Health, Civilization and the State: A History of Public Health from Ancient to Modern Times. London and New York: Routledge. ISBN 978-0415200363.

Crook, Tom (2016). Governing systems: modernity and the making of public health in England, 1830-1910. Oakland, California. ISBN 978-0-520-96454-9. OCLC 930786561.

Brown TM, Cueto M, Fee E (January 2006). "The World Health Organization and the transition from "international" to "global" public health". Am J Public Health. 96 (1): 62–72. doi:10.2105/AJPH.2004.050831. PMC 1470434. PMID 16322464.

Koplan JP, Bond TC, Merson MH, et al. (June 2009). "Towards a common definition of global health". Lancet. 373 (9679): 1993–5. CiteSeerX 10.1.1.610.7968. doi:10.1016/S0140-6736(09)60332-9. PMID 19493564. S2CID 6919716.

Valles, Sean A. (2018). Philosophy of population health : philosophy for a new public health era. London. ISBN 978-1-351-67078-4. OCLC 1035763221.

Joint Task Group on Public Health Human Resources; Advisory Committee on Health Delivery & Human Resources; Advisory Committee on Population Health & Health Security (2005). Building the public health workforce for the 21st century. Ottawa: Public Health Agency of Canada. OCLC 144167975.

Global Public-Private Partnership for Handwashing with Soap. Handwashing research Archived 16 December 2010 at the Wayback Machine, accessed 19 April 2011.

Wang, Fahui (2 January 2020). "Why public health needs GIS: a methodological overview". Annals of GIS. 26 (1): 1–12. doi:10.1080/19475683.2019.1702099. ISSN 1947-5683. PMC 7297184. PMID 32547679.

Holland, Stephen (2015). Public health ethics (Second ed.). Cambridge. ISBN 978-0-7456-6218-3. OCLC 871536632.

Fitzpatrick, Michael (4 January 2002). The Tyranny of Health: Doctors and the Regulation of Lifestyle. Routledge. ISBN 978-1-134-56346-3.

Fiona, Sim; Martin, McKee (1 September 2011). Issues In Public Health. McGraw-Hill Education (UK). ISBN 978-0-335-24422-5.

Fitzpatrick, Katie; Tinning, Richard (5 February 2014). Health Education: Critical perspectives. Routledge. ISBN 978-1-135-07214-8.

Zembylas, Michalinos (6 May 2021). Affect and the Rise of Right-Wing Populism: Pedagogies for the Renewal of Democratic Education. Cambridge University Press. ISBN 978-1-108-83840-5.

"The declines in infant mortality and fertility: Evidence from British cities in demographic transition". Retrieved 17 December 2012.

"10 facts on breastfeeding". World Health Organization. Retrieved 20 April 2011.

World Health Organization. Diabetes Fact Sheet N°312, January 2011. Accessed 19 April 2011.

The Lancet (2010). "Type 2 diabetes—time to change our approach". The Lancet. 375 (9733): 2193. doi:10.1016/S0140-6736(10)61011-2. PMID 20609952. S2CID 31166680.

World Health Organization. Obesity and overweight Fact sheet N°311, Updated June 2016. Accessed 19 April 2011.

"How can local authorities reduce obesity? Insights from NIHR research". NIHR Evidence. 19 May 2022.

"The U.S. Government and the World Health Organization". The Henry J. Kaiser Family Foundation. 24 January 2019. Archived from the original on 18 March 2020. Retrieved 18 March 2020.

"WHO Constitution, BASIC DOCUMENTS, Forty-ninth edition" (PDF). Archived (PDF) from the original on 1 April 2020.

"What we do". www.who.int. Archived from the original on 17 March 2020. Retrieved 17 March 2020.

Alkhuli, Muhammad Ali. English for Nursing and Medicine. دار الفلاح للنشر والتوزيع. ISBN 978-9957-552-36-7.

"Public health principles and neurological disorders". Neurological Disorders: Public Health Challenges (Report). Geneva: World Health Organization. 2006.

Hayes SL, Mann MK, Morgan FM, Kelly MJ, Weightman AL (17 October 2012). "Collaboration between local health and local government agencies for health improvement". Cochrane Database of Systematic Reviews. 10 (10): CD007825. doi:10.1002/14651858.CD007825.pub6. PMID 23076937.

Butcher, Lola (17 November 2020). "Pandemic puts all eyes on public health". Knowable Magazine. doi:10.1146/knowable-111720-1. Retrieved 2 March 2022.

World Health Organization. The role of WHO in public health, accessed 19 April 2011.

World Health Organization. Public health surveillance, accessed 19 April 2011.

Botchway, Stella; Hoang, Uy (2016). "Reflections on the United Kingdom's first public health film festival". Perspectives in Public Health. 136 (1): 23–24. doi:10.1177/1757913915619120. PMID 26702114. S2CID 21969020.

Valerie Curtis and Robert Aunger. "Motivational mismatch: evolved motives as the source of—and solution to—global public health problems". In Roberts, S. C. (2011). Roberts, S. Craig (ed.). Applied Evolutionary Psychology. Oxford University Press. doi:10.1093/acprof:oso/9780199586073.001.0001. ISBN 9780199586073.

Gillam Stephen; Yates, Jan; Badrinath, Padmanabhan (2007). Essential Public Health: theory and practice. Cambridge University Press. OCLC 144228591.

Pencheon, David; Guest, Charles; Melzer, David; Gray, JA Muir (2006). Pencheon, David (ed.). Oxford Handbook of Public Health Practice. Oxford University Press. OCLC 663666786.

Smith, Sarah; Sinclair, Don; Raine, Rosalind; Reeves, Barnarby (2005). Health Care Evaluation. Understanding Public Health. Open University Press. OCLC 228171855.

Sanderson, Colin J.; Gruen, Reinhold (2006). Analytical Models for Decision Making. Understanding Public Health. Open University Press. OCLC 182531015.

Byrd, Nick; Białek, Michał (2021). "Your Health vs. My Liberty: Philosophical beliefs dominated reflection and identifiable victim effects when predicting public health recommendation compliance during the COVID-19 pandemic". Cognition. 212: 104649. doi:10.1016/j.cognition.2021.104649. PMC 8599940. PMID 33756152.

United Nations. Press Conference on General Assembly Decision to Convene Summit in September 2011 on Non-Communicable Diseases. New York, 13 May 2010.

Prevention, CDC-Centers for Disease Control and (26 January 2021). "CDC - Malaria - Malaria Worldwide - Impact of Malaria". www.cdc.gov. Retrieved 19 October 2021.

"Fact sheet about Malaria". www.who.int. Retrieved 19 October 2021.

Organization, World Health (2010). Equity, Social Determinants and Public Health Programmes. World Health Organization. ISBN 9789241563970.

Richard G. Wilkinson; Michael G. Marmot, eds. (2003). The Solid Facts: Social Determinants of Health. WHO. OCLC 54966941.

Robert Huish and John M. Kirk (2007), "Cuban Medical Internationalism and the Development of the Latin American School of Medicine", Latin American Perspectives, 34; 77

Bendavid, Eran; Bhattacharya, Jay (2014). "The Relationship of Health Aid to Population Health Improvements". JAMA Internal Medicine. 174 (6): 881–887. doi:10.1001/jamainternmed.2014.292. PMC 4777302. PMID 24756557.

Twumasi, Patrick (1 April 1981). "Colonialism and international health: A study in social change in Ghana". Social Science & Medicine. Part B: Medical Anthropology. 15 (2): 147–151. doi:10.1016/0160-7987(81)90037-5. ISSN 0160-7987. PMID 7244686.

Afridi, Muhammad Asim; Ventelou, Bruno (1 March 2013). "Impact of health aid in developing countries: The public vs. the private channels". Economic Modelling. 31: 759–765. doi:10.1016/j.econmod.2013.01.009. ISSN 0264-9993.

"TDR | World Health Organization".

Shwank, Oliver. "Global Health Initiatives and Aid Effectiveness in the Health Sector" (PDF).

"2015 – United Nations sustainable development agenda". United Nations Sustainable Development. Retrieved 25 November 2015.

"Sustainable development goals – United Nations". United Nations Sustainable Development. Retrieved 25 November 2015.

"Health – United Nations Sustainable Development". United Nations Sustainable Development. Retrieved 25 November 2015.

"World Development Report". openknowledge.worldbank.org. Retrieved 25 November 2015.

Cosmacini, Giorgio (2005). Storia della medicina e della sanità in Italia: dalla peste nera ai giorni nostri. Bari: Laterza.

Shephard, Roy J. (2015). An illustrated history of health and fitness, from pre-history to our post-modern world. Cham. ISBN 978-3-319-11671-6. OCLC 897376985.

Berridge, V; (2016) Public Health: A Very Short Introduction. Oxford University Press, Oxford. ISBN 9780199688463

Chattopadhyay, Aparna (1968). "Hygienic Principles in the Regulations of Food Habits in the Dharma Sūtras". Nagarjun. 11: 194–99.

Leung, Angela Ki Che. "Hygiène et santé publique dans la Chine pré-moderne." In Les hygienists. Enjeux, modèles et practiques. Edited by Patrice Bourdelais, 343-71 (Paris: Belin, 2001)

Harvey, Herbert R. (1981). "Public Health in Aztec Society". Bulletin of the New York Academy of Medicine. 57 (2): 157–65. PMC 1805201. PMID 7011458.

"Gunyah, Goondie + Wurley: the Aboriginal architecture of Australia". Choice Reviews Online. 46 (1): 46–0090-46-0090. 1 September 2008. doi:10.5860/choice.46-0090. ISSN 0009-4978.

Gammage, Bill. (2014). Biggest Estate on Earth: How Aborigines made Australia. Allen & Unwin. ISBN 978-1-74269-352-1. OCLC 956710111.

Stearns, Justin K. (2011). Infectious ideas: contagion in premodern Islamic and Christian thought in the Western Mediterranean. Johns Hopkins Univ. Press. ISBN 978-0-8018-9873-0. OCLC 729944227.

Rawcliffe, Carole. (2019). Urban Bodies - Communal Health in Late Medieval English Towns and Cities. Boydell & Brewer, Limited. ISBN 978-1-78327-381-2. OCLC 1121393294.

Geltner, G. (2019). Roads to Health: Infrastructure and Urban Wellbeing in Later Medieval Italy. University of Pennsylvania Press. ISBN 978-0-8122-5135-7. OCLC 1076422219.

Varlik, Nükhet (22 July 2015). Plague and Empire in the Early Modern Mediterranean World. Cambridge University Press. doi:10.1017/cbo9781139004046. ISBN 978-1-139-00404-6. S2CID 197967256.

McVaugh, Michael R. "Arnald of Villanova's Regimen Almarie (Regimen Castra Sequentium) and Medieval Military Medicine." Viator 23 (1992): 201-14

Nicoud, Marilyn. (2013). Les régimes de santé au Moyen Âge Naissance et diffusion d'une écriture médicale en Italie et en France (XIIIe- XVe siècle). Publications de l'École française de Rome. ISBN 978-2-7283-1006-7. OCLC 960812022.

Ibn Riḍwān, ʻAlī Abū al-Ḥasan al-Miṣrī (1984) [11th century]. Gamal, Adil S. (ed.). Medieval Islamic medicine: Ibn Riḍwān's treatise "On the prevention of bodily ills in Egypt. Translated by Dols, Michael W. University of California Press. OCLC 469624320.

L.J. Rather, 'The Six Things Non-Natural: A Note on the Origins and Fate of a Doctrine and a Phrase', Clio Medica, iii (1968)

Luis García-Ballester, 'On the Origins of the Six Non-Natural Things in Galen', in Jutta Kollesch and Diethard Nickel (eds.), Galen und das hellenistische Erbe: Verhandlungen des IV. Internationalen Galen-Symposiums veranstaltet vom Institut für Geschichte der Medizin am

Bereich Medizin (Charité) der Humboldt-Universität zu Berlin 18.-20. September 1989 (Stuttgart, 1993)

Janna Coomans and G. Geltner, 'On the Street and in the Bath-House: Medieval Galenism in Action?' Anuario de Estudios Medievales, xliii (2013)

Israelovich, Ido. "Medical Care in the Roman Army during the High Empire." In Popular Medicine in Graeco-Roman Antiquity: Explorations. Edited by William V. Harris, 126-46 (Leiden: Brill, 2016)

Geltner, G. (January 2019). "In the Camp and on the March: Military Manuals as Sources for Studying Premodern Public Health". Medical History. 63 (1): 44–60. doi:10.1017/mdh.2018.62. ISSN 0025-7273. PMC 8670759. PMID 30556517.

Harvey, Barbara F. (2002). Living and dying in England, 1100-1540: the monastic experience. Clarendon Press. ISBN 0-19-820431-0. OCLC 612358999.

Agostino Paravicini Bagliani, 'La Mobilità della Curia romana nel Secolo XIII: Riflessi locali', in Società e Istituzioni dell'Italia comunale: l'Esempio di Perugia (Secoli XII-XIV), 2 vols. (Perugia, 1988)

Coomans, Janna (February 2019). "The king of dirt: public health and sanitation in late medieval Ghent". Urban History. 46 (1): 82–105. doi:10.1017/S096392681800024X. ISSN 0963-9268.

Glick, T.F. "New Perspectives on the Hisba and its Hispanic Derivatives." Al-Qantara 13 (1992): 475-89

Kinzelbach, Annemarie. "Infection, Contagion, and Public Health in Late Medieval German Imperial Towns." Journal of the History of Medicine and Allied Sciences 61 (2006): 369-89

Jørgensen, Dolly. "Cooperative Sanitation: Managing Streets and Gutters in Late Medieval England and Scandinavia." Technology and Culture 49 (2008): 547-67

Henderson, John. "Public Health, Pollution and the Problem of Waste Disposal in Early Modern Tuscany." In Le interazioni fra economia e ambiente biologico nell'Europa preindustriale. Secc. XIII-XVIII. Edited by Simonetta Cavaciocchi, 373-82 (Florence: Firenze University Press, 2010)

Nutton, Vivian. "Continuity or Rediscovery? The City Physician in Classical Antiquity and Mediaeval Italy." In The Town and State Physician in Europe. Edited by Andrew W. Russell, 9-46. (Wolfenbüttel: Herzog August Bibliothek, 1981)

Rawcliffe, Carole. (2009). Leprosy in medieval England. The Boydell Press. ISBN 978-1-84383-454-0. OCLC 884314023.

Demaitre, Luke E. (2007). Leprosy in premodern medicine: a malady of the whole body. Johns Hopkins University Press. ISBN 978-0-8018-8613-3. OCLC 799983230.

Adam Sabra. (2006). Poverty and charity in medieval islam: mamluk egypt, 1250-1517. Cambridge University Press. ISBN 0-521-03474-4. OCLC 712129032.

Cascoigne, Alison L. "The Water Supply of Tinnīs: Public Amenities and Private Investments." In Cities in the Pre-Modern Islamic World: The Urban Impact of Religion, State and Society. Edited by Amira K. Bennison and Alison L. Gascoigne, 161-76 (London: Routledge, 2007)

Horden, Peregrine. "Ritual and Public Health in the Early Medieval City." In Body and City: Histories of Urban Public Health. Edited by Sally Sheard and Helen Power, 17-40 (Aldershot, UK: Ashgate, 2000)

Falcón, Isabel. "Aprovisionamiento y sanidad en Zaragoza en el siglo XV." Acta Historica et Archaeologica Mediaeval 19 (1998): 127-44

Duccio Balestracci, 'The Regulation of Public Health in Italian Medieval Towns', in Helmut Hundsbichler, Gerhard Jaritz and Thomas Kühtreiber (eds.), Die Vielfalt der Dinge: Neue Wege zur Analyse mittelaltericher Sachkultur (Vienna, 1998)

Ewert, Ulf Christian. "Water, Public Hygiene and Fire Control in Medieval Towns: Facing Collective Goods Problems while Ensuring the Quality of Life." Historical Social Research/Historische Sozialforschung 32 (2007): 222-52

Anja Petaros et al., 'Public Health Problems in the Medieval Statutes of Croatian Adriatic Coastal Towns: From Public Morality to Public Health', Journal of Religion and Health, lii (2013)

Skelton, Leona J. (2016). Sanitation in urban Britain, 1560-1700. ISBN 978-1-317-21789-3. OCLC 933433427.

Carmichael, Ann G. "Plague Legislation in the Italian Renaissance." Bulletin of the History of Medicine 7 (1983): 508-25

Geltner, G. (2019). "The Path to Pistoia: Urban Hygiene Before the Black Death". Past & Present. 246: 3–33. doi:10.1093/pastj/gtz028.

Blažina-Tomić, Zlata; Blažina, Vesna (2015). Expelling the plague: the health office and the implementation of quarantine in Dubrovnik, 1377-1533. ISBN 978-0-7735-4539-7. OCLC 937888436.

Gall, Gabriella Eva Cristina, Stephan Lautenschlager and Homayoun C. Bagheri. "Quarantine as a Public Health Measure against an Emerging Infectious Disease: Syphilis in Zurich at the Dawn of the Modern Era

(1496-1585)." Hygiene and Infection Control 11 (2016): 1-10

Cipolla, Carlo M. (1973). Cristofano and the plague: a study in the history of public health in the age of Galileo. University of California Press. ISBN 0-520-02341-2. OCLC 802505260.

Carmichael, Ann G. (2014) [1986]. Plague and the poor in Renaissance Florence. ISBN 978-1-107-63436-7. OCLC 906714501.

Cohn, Samuel K. (2012). Cultures of plague: medical thinking at the end of the Renaissance. Oxford University Press. ISBN 978-0-19-957402-5. OCLC 825731416.

Rhodes, Philip; Bryant, John H. (20 May 2019). "Public Health". Encyclopædia Britannica.

Carruthers, G. Barry; Carruthers, Lesley A. (2005). A History of Britain's Hospitals. Book Guild Publishers. ISBN 9781857769050.

Vale, Brian. "The Conquest of Scurvy in the Royal Navy 1793–1800: A Challenge to Current Orthodoxy". The Mariners' Mirror, volume 94, number 2, May 2008, pp. 160–175.

Selwyn, S (1966), "Sir John Pringle: hospital reformer, moral philosopher and pioneer of antiseptics", Medical History (published July 1966), vol. 10, no. 3, pp. 266–74, doi:10.1017/s0025727300011133, PMC 1033606, PMID 5330009

Amanda J. Thomas (2010). The Lambeth cholera outbreak of 1848–1849: the setting, causes, course and aftermath of an epidemic in London. McFarland. pp. 55–6. ISBN 978-0-7864-3989-8.

Margaret Stacey (1 June 2004). The Sociology of Health and Healing. Taylor and Francis. p. 69. ISBN 978-0-203-38004-8.

Samuel Edward Finer (1952). The Life and Times of Sir Edwin Chadwick. Methuen. pp. 424–5. ISBN 978-0-416-17350-5.

Ashton, John; Ubido, Janet (1991). "The Healthy City and the Ecological Idea" (PDF). Journal of the Society for the Social History of Medicine. 4 (1): 173–181. doi:10.1093/shm/4.1.173. PMID 11622856. Archived from the original (PDF) on 24 December 2013. Retrieved 8 July 2013.

Chadwick, Edwin (1842). "Chadwick's Report on Sanitary Conditions". excerpt from Report...from the Poor Law Commissioners on an Inquiry into the Sanitary Conditions of the Labouring Population of Great Britain (pp. 369–372) (online source). added by Laura Del Col: to The Victorian Web. Retrieved 8 November 2009.

Chadwick, Edwin (1843). Report on the Sanitary Condition of the Labouring Population of Great Britain. A Supplementary Report on the results of a Special Inquiry into The Practice of Interment in Towns. London:

Printed by R. Clowes & Sons, for Her Majesty's Stationery Office. Full text at Internet Archive (archive.org)

Brunton, Deborah (2008). The Politics of Vaccination: Practice and Policy in England, Wales, Ireland, and Scotland, 1800-1874. University Rochester Press. p. 39. ISBN 9781580460361.

"Decline of Infant Mortality in England and Wales, 1871–1948: a Medical Conundrum". Retrieved 17 December 2012.

Mooney, Graham (2015). Intrusive Interventions: Public Health, Domestic Space, and Infectious Disease Surveillance in England, 1840–1914. Rochester, NY: University of Rochester Press. ISBN 9781580465274.

United States Public Health Service, Municipal Health Department Practice for the Year 1923 (Public Health Bulletin # 164, July 1926), pp. 348, 357, 364

https://www.ushmm.org/m/pdfs/07192004-nazi-racial-hygiene-bachrach.pdf[bare URL PDF]

Vinten-Johansen, Peter, et al. (2003). Cholera, Chloroform, and the Science of Medicine: A Life of John Snow. Oxford University Press. ISBN 0-19-513544-X

Johnson, Steven (2006). The Ghost Map: The Story of London's Most Terrifying Epidemic – and How it Changed Science, Cities and the Modern World. Riverhead Books. ISBN 1-59448-925-4

Miquel Porta (2014). A Dictionary of Epidemiology (6th ed.). New York: Oxford University Press. ISBN 978-0-19-997673-7.

":: Laboc Hospital – A Noble Prize Winner's Workplace". easternpanorama.in. Archived from the original on 5 November 2013. Retrieved 11 July 2013.

Edward Marriott (1966) in "Plague. A Story of Science, Rivalry and the Scourge That Won't Go Away" ISBN 978-1-4223-5652-4

Ronn F. Pineo, "Public Health" in Encyclopedia of Latin American History and Culture, vol. 4, p. 481. New York: Charles Scribner's Sons 1996.

Pierce J.R., J, Writer. 2005. Yellow Jack: How Yellow Fever Ravaged America and Walter Reed Discovered its Deadly Secrets. John Wiley and Sons. ISBN 0-471-47261-1

Pineo, "Public Health", p. 481.

"Achievements in Public Health, 1900–1999" (PDF). Morbidity and Mortality Weekly Report. Vol. 48, no. 50. U.S. Department of Health & Human Services. 24 December 1999.

Public Health Agency of Canada. Canadian Public Health Workforce Core Competencies, accessed 19 April 2011.

White, Franklin (2013). "The Imperative of Public Health Education: A Global Perspective". Medical Principles and Practice. 22 (6): 515–529. doi:10.1159/000354198. PMC 5586806. PMID 23969636.

Welch, William H.; Rose, Wickliffe (1915). Institute of Hygiene: Being a report by Dr. William H. Welch and Wickliffe Rose to the General Education Board, Rockefeller Foundation (Report). pp. 660–668. reprinted in Fee, Elizabeth (1992). The Welch-Rose Report: Blueprint for Public Health Education in America (PDF). Washington, DC: Delta Omega Honorary Public Health Society. Archived from the original (PDF) on 7 May 2012.

Patel, Kant; Rushefsky, Mark E.; McFarlane, Deborah R. (2005). The Politics of Public Health in the United States. M.E. Sharpe. p. 91. ISBN 978-0-7656-1135-2.

Brandt AM, Gardner M (2000). "Antagonism and accommodation: interpreting the relationship between public health and medicine in the United States during the 20th century". American Journal of Public Health. 90 (5): 707–15. doi:10.2105/AJPH.90.5.707. PMC 1446218. PMID 10800418.

White, Kerr L. (1991). Healing the schism: Epidemiology, medicine, and the public's health. New York: Springer-Verlag. ISBN 978-0-387-97574-0.

Darnell, Regna (2008). Histories of anthropology annual. University of Nebraska Press. p. 36. ISBN 978-0-8032-6664-3.

Dyer, John Percy (1966). Tulane: the biography of a university, 1834-1965. Harper & Row. p. 136.

Burrow, Gerard N. (2002). A history of Yale's School of Medicine: passing torches to others. New Haven: Yale University Press. ISBN 9780300132885. OCLC 182530966.

Education of the Physician: International Dimensions. Education Commission for Foreign Medical Graduates., Association of American Medical Colleges. Meeting. (1984 : Chicago, Ill), p. v.

Milton Terris, "The Profession of Public Health", Conference on Education, Training, and the Future of Public Health. 22–24 March 1987. Board on Health Care Services. Washington, DC: National Academy Press, p. 53.

Sheps, Cecil G. (1973). "Schools of Public Health in Transition". The Milbank Memorial Fund Quarterly. Health and Society. 51 (4): 462–468. doi:10.2307/3349628. JSTOR 3349628.

Kar, Snehendu B. (18 May 2018). Empowerment of Women for Promoting Health and Quality of Life. Oxford University Press. p. 69. ISBN 978-0-19-938467-9.

"Schools of Public Health and Public Health Programs" (PDF). Council on Education for Public Health. 11 March 2011. Archived from the original (PDF) on 11 June 2012. Retrieved 30 March 2011.

Berke, Olaf; Sobkowich, Kurtis; Bernardo, Theresa M. (1 November 2020). "Celebration day: 400th birthday of John Graunt, citizen scientist of London". Environmental Health Review. 63 (3): 67–69. doi:10.5864/d2020-018. ISSN 0319-6771. S2CID 228938397.

Winkelstein, Warren (July 2008). "Lemuel Shattuck: Architect of American Public Health". Epidemiology. 19 (4): 634. doi:10.1097/EDE.0b013e31817307f2. ISSN 1044-3983. PMID 18552594.

Halliday, Stephen (2013). The Great Stink of London: Sir Joseph Bazalgette and the Cleansing of the Victorian Metropolis. The History Press. ISBN 978-0752493787.

Beitsch, Leslie M.; Yeager, Valerie A.; Moran, John (18 March 2015). "Deciphering the Imperative: Translating Public Health Quality Improvement into Organizational Performance Management Gains". Annual Review of Public Health. 36 (1): 273–287. doi:10.1146/annurev-publhealth-031914-122810. PMID 25494050.

Parry, Manon S. (April 2006). "Sara Josephine Baker (1873–1945)". American Journal of Public Health. 96 (4): 620–621. doi:10.2105/AJPH.2005.079145. ISSN 0090-0036. PMC 1470556.

Mackie, Elizabeth M; Scott Wilson, T. (12 November 1994). "Obituary N.I.Wattie". British Medical Journal. 309: 1297.

"Canada: International Health Care System Profiles". international.commonwealthfund.org. Retrieved 25 May 2020.

Pineo, "Public Health", p. 483.

Hanni Jalil, "Curing a Sick Nation: Public Health and Citizenship in Colombia, 1930–1940." PhD dissertation, University of California, Santa Barbara 2015.

Nicole Pacino, "Prescription for a Nation: Public Health in Post-Revolutionary Bolivia, 1952–1964." PhD dissertation, University of California, Santa Barbara 2013.

"CDC Global Health – Ghana". www.cdc.gov. Retrieved 9 April 2018.

Agyepong, Irene Akua; Manderson, Lenore (January 1999). "Mosquito Avoidance and Bed Net Use in the Greater Accra Region, Ghana". Journal of Biosocial Science. 31 (1): 79–92. doi:10.1017/S0021932099000796. ISSN 1469-7599. PMID 10081239.

"Ghana Demographic and Health Survey 2014" (PDF). Retrieved 18 May 2020.

Allan Mitchell, The Divided Path: The German Influence on Social Reform in France After 1870 (1991) pp 252–75 excerpt

Martha L. Hildreth, Doctors, Bureaucrats & Public Health in France, 1888–1902 (1987)

Alisa Klaus, Every Child a Lion: The Origins of Maternal & Infant Health Policy in the United States & France, 1890–1920 (1993).

Ann-Louise Shapiro, "Private Rights, Public Interest, and Professional Jurisdiction: The French Public Health Law of 1902." Bulletin of the History of Medicine 54.1 (1980): 4+

Donald Cooper, Epidemic Disease in Mexico City, 1761–1813: An Administrative, Social, and Medical History. Austin: University of Texas Press 1965.

Agostoni, Claudia. Monuments of Progress: Modernization and Public Health in Mexico City, 1876–1910. Calgary: University of Calgary Press; Boulder: University of Colorado Press; Mexico City: Instituto de Investigaciones Históricos 2003.

Soto Laveaga, Gabriela; Agostoni, Claudia (20 April 2011), Beezley, William H. (ed.), "Science and Public Health in the Century of Revolution", A Companion to Mexican History and Culture, Oxford, UK: Wiley-Blackwell, pp. 561–574, doi:10.1002/9781444340600.ch33, ISBN 978-1-4443-4060-0

Alexander, Anna Rose, City on Fire: Technology, Social Change, and the Hazards of Progress in Mexico City, 1860–1910. Pittsburgh: University of Pittsburgh Press 2016.

Pilcher, Jeffrey M. The Sausage Rebellion: Public Health, Private Enterprise, and Meat in Mexico City, 1890–1917. Albuquerque: University of New Mexico Press 2006.

Pani, Alberto J. (1916). La higiene en México (in Spanish). Mexico: Imprenta de J. Ballescá.

Bliss, Katherine (1 February 1999). "The Science of Redemption: Syphilis, Sexual Promiscuity, and Reformism in Revolutionary Mexico City". Hispanic American Historical Review. 79 (1): 1–40. doi:10.1215/00182168-79.1.1. PMID 21162337.

Ernesto Aréchiga Córdoba, "Educación, propaganda o 'Dictadura sanitaria'. Estrategias discursivas de higiene y salubridad pública en el

México posrevolucionario, 1917–1934". Dynamis 25, 2005, pp. 117–143.

Anthony J. Mazzaferri, "Public Health and Social Revolution in Mexico." PhD dissertation, Kent State University 1968.

David Sowell, Medicine on the Periphery: Public Health in Yucatán, 1870–1960. Lanham: Lexington Books 2015.

Leider, Jonathon P.; Resnick, Beth; Bishai, David; Scutchfield, F. Douglas (1 April 2018). "How Much Do We Spend? Creating Historical Estimates of Public Health Expenditures in the United States at the Federal, State, and Local Levels". Annual Review of Public Health. 39 (1): 471–487. doi:10.1146/annurev-publhealth-040617-013455. ISSN 0163-7525. PMID 29346058.

Himmelstein, David U.; Woolhandler, Steffie (January 2016). "Public Health's Falling Share of US Health Spending". American Journal of Public Health. 106 (1): 56–57. doi:10.2105/AJPH.2015.302908. PMC 4695931. PMID 26562115.

Alfonso, Y. Natalia; Leider, Jonathon P.; Resnick, Beth; McCullough, J. Mac; Bishai, David (1 April 2021). "US Public Health Neglected: Flat Or Declining Spending Left States Ill Equipped To Respond To COVID-19". Health Affairs. 40 (4): 664–671. doi:10.1377/hlthaff.2020.01084. ISSN 0278-2715. PMID 33764801. S2CID 232367227.

Institute of Medicine (2012). For the Public's Health: Investing in a Healthier Future. Washington, DC: The National Academies Press. p. 2. doi:10.17226/13268. ISBN 978-0-309-22107-8. PMID 24830052.

"Health Care Costs Accounted for 17.7 Percent of GDP in 2018". California Health Care Foundation. 2 June 2020. Retrieved 2 March 2022.

Nunn, Ryan; Parsons, Jana; Shambaugh, Jay (10 March 2020). "A dozen facts about the economics of the US health-care system". Brookings Institute. Retrieved 2 March 2022.

Wallace, Megan; Sharfstein, Joshua M. (6 January 2022). "The Patchwork U.S. Public Health System". New England Journal of Medicine. 386 (1): 1–4. doi:10.1056/NEJMp2104881. PMID 34979071. S2CID 245640052.

"Explore Public Health Funding in the United States | 2021 Annual Report". America's Health Rankings. Retrieved 2 March 2022.

"GHJP Report Calls for Reinvestment to Revive Public Health in the U.S." Yale Law School. 7 June 2021. Retrieved 2 March 2022.

Eager, William; Herman, David; House, Margaret; Robinson, Leah; Williams, Christopher (2021). Confronting a legacy of scarcity: a plan for America's reinvestment in U.S. public health (PDF). Yale School of Public Health.

"The Impact of Chronic Underfunding on America's Public Health System: Trends, Risks, and Recommendations, 2021". Trust for America's Health. 7 May 2021. Retrieved 2 March 2022.

Porta, Miquel (2014). A Dictionary of Epidemiology (6th ed.). New York: Oxford University Press. ISBN 978-0-19-997673-7. Retrieved 16 July 2014.

Nutter, Jr., F.W. (1999). "Understanding the interrelationships between botanical, human, and veterinary epidemiology: the Ys and Rs of it all". Ecosystem Health. 5 (3): 131–40. doi:10.1046/j.1526-0992.1999.09922.x.

Hippocrates (~200 BC). Airs, Waters, Places.

Carol Buck, Alvaro Llopis; Enrique Nájera; Milton Terris (1998) The Challenge of Epidemiology: Issues and Selected Readings. Scientific Publication No. 505. Pan American Health Organization. Washington, DC. p. 3.

Alfredo Morabia (2004). A history of epidemiologic methods and concepts. Birkhäuser. p. 93. ISBN 978-3-7643-6818-0.

Historical Developments in Epidemiology. Chapter 2. Jones & Bartlett Learning LLC.

Ray M. Merrill (2010). Introduction to Epidemiology. Jones & Bartlett Learning. p. 24. ISBN 978-0-7637-6622-1.

Merril, Ray M., PhD, MPH. (2010): An Introduction to Epidemiology, Fifth Edition. Chapter 2: "Historic Developments in Epidemiology". Jones and Bartlett Publishing

"Changing Concepts: Background to Epidemiology" (PDF). Duncan & Associates. Archived from the original (PDF) on 25 July 2011. Retrieved 3 February 2008.

Joseph, P Byre (2012). Encyclopedia of the Black Death. ABC-CLIO. p. 76. ISBN 978-1598842548. Retrieved 24 February 2019.

Guobin, Xu; Yanhui, Chen; Lianhua, Xu (2018). Introduction to Chinese Culture: Cultural History, Arts, Festivals and Rituals. Springer. p. 70. ISBN 978-9811081569. Retrieved 24 February 2019.

"SARS: Clinical Trials on Treatment Using a Combination of Traditional Chinese Medicine and Western Medicine". World Health Organization. Archived from the original on 8 June 2018. Retrieved 24 February 2019.

Doctor John Snow Blames Water Pollution for Cholera Epidemic, by David Vachon UCLA Department of Epidemiology, School of Public Health May & June 2005

John Snow, Father of Epidemiology NPR Talk of the Nation. 24 September 2004

The Importance of Snow. Gro Harlem Brundtland, M.D., M:P.H.former Director-General, World Health Organization. Geneva, Switzerland Talk, Washington, DC, 28 October 1998

Dr. John Snow. John Snow, Inc. and JSI Research & Training Institute, Inc.

Johnson, Steven, The ghost map : [the story of London's most terrifying epidemic – and how it changed science, cities, and the modern world], OCLC 1062993385, retrieved 16 September 2020

Krishna; Kr (May 2019). "Education Consultancy". Krishna.

Ólöf Garðarsdóttir; Loftur Guttormsson (25 August 2009). "Public health measures against neonatal tetanus on the island of Vestmannaeyjar (Iceland) during the 19th century". The History of the Family. 14 (3): 266–79. doi:10.1016/j.hisfam.2009.08.004. S2CID 72505045.[verification needed]

Statisticians of the centuries. By C. C. Heyde, Eugene Senet

Anderson Gray McKendrick Archived 22 August 2011 at the Wayback Machine

Statistical methods in epidemiology: Karl Pearson, Ronald Ross, Major Greenwood and Austin Bradford Hill, 1900–1945. Trust Centre for the History of Medicine at UCL, London

"Origins and early development of the case-control study" (PDF). Archived from the original (PDF) on 18 January 2017. Retrieved 31 August 2013.

Mueller LM (2019). "Cancer in the tropics: geographical pathology and the formation of cancer epidemiology". BioSocieties. 14 (4): 512–528. doi:10.1057/s41292-019-00152-w. hdl:1721.1/128433. S2CID 181518236.

Ogino S, Fuchs CS, Giovannucci E (2012). "How many molecular subtypes? Implications of the unique tumor principle in personalized medicine". Expert Rev Mol Diagn. 12 (6): 621–28. doi:10.1586/erm.12.46. PMC 3492839. PMID 22845482.

Ogino S, Lochhead P, Chan AT, Nishihara R, Cho E, Wolpin BM, Meyerhardt JA, Meissner A, Schernhammer ES, Fuchs CS, Giovannucci E (2013). "Molecular pathological epidemiology of epigenetics: Emerging integrative science to analyze environment, host, and disease". Mod Pathol. 26 (4): 465–84. doi:10.1038/modpathol.2012.214. PMC 3637979. PMID 23307060.

Ogino S, King EE, Beck AH, Sherman ME, Milner DA, Giovannucci E (2012). "Interdisciplinary education to integrate pathology and epidemiology: Towards molecular and population-level health science". Am J Epidemiol. 176 (8): 659–67. doi:10.1093/aje/kws226. PMC 3571252. PMID

22935517.

Ogino S, Stampfer M (2010). "Lifestyle factors and microsatellite instability in colorectal cancer: the evolving field of molecular pathological epidemiology". J Natl Cancer Inst. 102 (6): 365–67. doi:10.1093/jnci/djq031. PMC 2841039. PMID 20208016.

Ogino S, Chan AT, Fuchs CS, Giovannucci E (2011). "Molecular pathological epidemiology of colorectal neoplasia: an emerging transdisciplinary and interdisciplinary field". Gut. 60 (3): 397–411. doi:10.1136/gut.2010.217182. PMC 3040598. PMID 21036793.

Field AE, Camargo CA, Ogino S (2013). "The merits of subtyping obesity: one size does not fit all". JAMA. 310 (20): 2147–48. doi:10.1001/jama.2013.281501. PMID 24189835.

Curtin K, Slattery ML, Samowitz WS (2011). "CpG island methylation in colorectal cancer: past, present and future". Pathology Research International. 2011: 902674. doi:10.4061/2011/902674. PMC 3090226. PMID 21559209.

Hughes LA, Khalid-de Bakker CA, Smits KM, den Brandt PA, Jonkers D, Ahuja N, Herman JG, Weijenberg MP, van Engeland M (2012). "The CpG island methylator phenotype in colorectal cancer: Progress and problems". Biochim Biophys Acta. 1825 (1): 77–85. doi:10.1016/j.bbcan.2011.10.005. PMID 22056543.

Ku CS, Cooper DN, Wu M, Roukos DH, Pawitan Y, Soong R, Iacopetta B (2012). "Gene discovery in familial cancer syndromes by exome sequencing: prospects for the elucidation of familial colorectal cancer type X." Mod Pathol. 25 (8): 1055–68. doi:10.1038/modpathol.2012.62. PMID 22522846.

Chia WK, Ali R, Toh HC (2012). "Aspirin as adjuvant therapy for colorectal cancer-reinterpreting paradigms". Nat Rev Clin Oncol. 9 (10): 561–70. doi:10.1038/nrclinonc.2012.137. PMID 22910681. S2CID 7425809.

Spitz MR, Caporaso NE, Sellers TA (2012). "Integrative cancer epidemiology – the next generation". Cancer Discov. 2 (12): 1087–90. doi:10.1158/2159-8290.cd-12-0424. PMC 3531829. PMID 23230187.

Zaidi N, Lupien L, Kuemmerle NB, Kinlaw WB, Swinnen JV, Smans K (2013). "Lipogenesis and lipolysis: The pathways exploited by the cancer cells to acquire fatty acids". Prog Lipid Res. 52 (4): 585–89. doi:10.1016/j.plipres.2013.08.005. PMC 4002264. PMID 24001676.

Ikramuddin S, Livingston EH (2013). "New Insights on Bariatric Surgery Outcomes". JAMA. 310 (22): 2401–02. doi:10.1001/jama.2013.280927. PMID 24189645.

Little TJ, Allen JE, Babayan SA, Matthews KR, Colegrave N (2012). "Harnessing evolutionary biology to combat infectious disease". Nature Medicine. 18 (2): 217–20. doi:10.1038/nm.2572. PMC 3712261. PMID 22310693.

Pybus OG, Fraser C, Rambaut A (2013). "Evolutionary epidemiology: preparing for an age of genomic plenty". Phil Trans R Soc B. 368 (1614): 20120193. doi:10.1098/rstb.2012.0193. PMC 3678320. PMID 23382418.

Wiemken, Timothy L.; Kelley, Robert R. (2020). "Machine Learning in Epidemiology and Health Outcomes Research". Annual Review of Public Health. 41: 21–36. doi:10.1146/annurev-publhealth-040119-094437. PMID 31577910.

Bi, Qifang; Goodman, Katherine E.; Kaminsky, Joshua; Lessler, Justin (2019). "What is Machine Learning? A Primer for the Epidemiologist". American Journal of Epidemiology. 188 (12): 2222–2239. doi:10.1093/aje/kwz189. PMID 31509183.

"Principles of Epidemiology." Key Concepts in Public Health. London: Sage UK, 2009. Credo Reference. 1 August 2011. Web. 30 September 2012.

Hennekens, Charles H.; Julie E. Buring (1987). Mayrent, Sherry L. (ed.). Epidemiology in Medicine. Lippincott, Williams and Wilkins. ISBN 978-0-316-35636-7.

Woodward, James (2010). "Causation in biology: stability, specificity, and the choice of levels of explanation". Biology & Philosophy. 25 (3): 287–318. doi:10.1007/s10539-010-9200-z. S2CID 42625229 – via SpringerLink.

Rothman, Kenneth J. (1986). Modern Epidemiology. Boston/Toronto: Little, Brown and Company. ISBN 978-0-316-75776-8.

Rothman, Kenneth J. (2012). Epidemiology : An introduction (2nd ed.). New York, NY: Oxford University Press. p. 24. ISBN 978-0-19-975455-7. OCLC 750986180.

Hill, Austin Bradford (1965). "The Environment and Disease: Association or Causation?". Proceedings of the Royal Society of Medicine. 58 (5): 295–300. doi:10.1177/003591576505800503. PMC 1898525. PMID 14283879.

Phillips, Carl V.; Karen J. Goodman (October 2004). "The missed lessons of Sir Austin Bradford Hill". Epidemiologic Perspectives and Innovations. 1 (3): 3. doi:10.1186/1742-5573-1-3. PMC 524370. PMID 15507128.

Green, Michael D.; D. Michal Freedman, and Leon Gordis. Reference Guide on Epidemiology (PDF). Federal Judicial Centre. Archived from the original (PDF) on 27 February 2008. Retrieved 3 February 2008.

Neil Myburgh; Debra Jackson. "Measuring Health and Disease I: Introduction to Epidemiology". Archived from the original on 1 August 2011.

Retrieved 16 December 2011.

Smetanin, P.; P. Kobak (October 2005). Interdisciplinary Cancer Risk Management: Canadian Life and Economic Impacts. 1st International Cancer Control Congress (PDF).

Smetanin, P.; P. Kobak (July 2006). A Population-Based Risk Management Framework for Cancer Control. The International Union Against Cancer Conference. Archived from the original (PDF) on 2 February 2014.

Smetanin, P.; P. Kobak (July 2005). Selected Canadian Life and Economic Forecast Impacts of Lung Cancer. 11th World Conference on Lung Cancer. Archived from the original (PDF) on 2 February 2014.

WHO, "Health topics: Epidemiology." Accessed: 30 October 2017.

Miquel Porta. A Dictionary of Epidemiology. http://global.oup.com/academic/product/a-dictionary-of-epidemiology-9780199976737?cc=us&lang=en 6th edition, New York, 2014 Oxford University Press ISBN 978-0-19-997673-7 Accessed: 30 October 2017.

Prudhon, C & Spiegel, P. "A review of methodology and analysis of nutrition and mortality surveys conducted in humanitarian emergencies from October 1993 to April 2004" Emerging Themes in Epidemiology 2007, 4:10. http://www.ete-online.com/content/4/1/10 Accessed: 30 October 2017.

Roberts, B et al. "A new method to estimate mortality in crisis-affected and resource-poor settings: validation study." International Journal of Epidemiology 2010; 39:1584–96. Accessed: 30 October 2017.

Ioannidis, J. P. A.; Tarone, R.; McLaughlin, J. K. (2011). "The False-positive to False-negative Ratio in Epidemiologic Studies". Epidemiology. 22 (4): 450–56. doi:10.1097/EDE.0b013e31821b506e. PMID 21490505. S2CID 42756884.

Hernán, M. A.; Hernández-Díaz, S.; Robins, J. M. (2004). "A structural approach to selection bias". Epidemiology. 15 (5): 615–25. doi:10.1097/01.ede.0000135174.63482.43. PMID 15308962. S2CID 1373077. [1] Archived 29 August 2017 at the Wayback Machine 24

Rothman, K. (2002). Epidemiology: An Introduction. Oxford: Oxford University Press. ISBN 978-0195135541.

Greenland S, Morgenstern H (2001). "Confounding in Health Research". Annu. Rev. Public Health. 22: 189–212. doi:10.1146/annurev.publhealth.22.1.189. PMID 11274518. S2CID 4647751.

"Public Health Studies". Public Health Studies at Johns Hopkins. Retrieved 13 April 2017.

Hiro, Brian. "Ask the Expert: The Epidemiology of COVID-19". SCUSM. Retrieved 11 June 2020.

"Pollution – Definition from the Merriam-Webster Online Dictionary". Merriam-Webster. 2010-08-13. Retrieved 2010-08-26.

Beil, Laura (15 November 2017). "Pollution killed 9 million people in 2015". Science News. Retrieved 1 December 2017.

Jump up to:a b Carrington, Damian (October 20, 2017). "Global pollution kills 9m a year and threatens 'survival of human societies'". The Guardian. Retrieved October 20, 2017.

"System of Registries | US EPA". sor.epa.gov. Retrieved 2022-05-01.

"UNdata | glossary". data.un.org. Retrieved 2022-05-01.

Concerns about MTBE from U.S. EPA website

Aboyeji, Oyebanji Oluseun (2013-12-01). "Freshwater Pollution in Some Nigerian Local Communities, Causes, Consequences and Probable Solutions". Academic Journal of Interdisciplinary Studies. doi:10.5901/ajis.2013.v2n13p111.

Englande, A.J.; Krenkel, Peter; Shamas, J. (2015), "Wastewater Treatment &Water Reclamation☆", Reference Module in Earth Systems and Environmental Sciences, Elsevier, pp. B9780124095489095087, doi:10.1016/b978-0-12-409548-9.09508-7, ISBN 978-0-12-409548-9, PMC 7158167, retrieved 2022-06-07

Ahmed, Jebin; Thakur, Abhijeet; Goyal, Arun (2021), Shah, Maulin P (ed.), "CHAPTER 1. Industrial Wastewater and Its Toxic Effects", Chemistry in the Environment, Cambridge: Royal Society of Chemistry, pp. 1–14, doi:10.1039/9781839165399-00001, ISBN 978-1-83916-279-4, retrieved 2022-06-07

Aqeel, Muhammad; Jamil, Mohd.; Yusoff, Ismail (2014-03-26), Hernandez Soriano, Maria C. (ed.), "Soil Contamination, Risk Assessment and Remediation", Environmental Risk Assessment of Soil Contamination, InTech, doi:10.5772/57287, ISBN 978-953-51-1235-8, retrieved 2022-06-07

"Volcanic gases can be harmful to health, vegetation and infrastructure". United States Geologic Survey. Retrieved 2022-05-07.

Trejos, Erika M.; Silva, Luis F. O.; Hower, James C.; Flores, Eriko M. M.; González, Carlos Mario; Pachón, Jorge E.; Aristizábal, Beatriz H. (2021-03-01). "Volcanic emissions and atmospheric pollution: A study of nanoparticles". Geoscience Frontiers. 12 (2): 746–755. doi:10.1016/j.gsf.2020.08.013. ISSN 1674-9871. S2CID 224936937.

"Wildfires". World Health Organization. Retrieved 2022-05-08.

Environmental Performance Report 2001 Archived 2007-11-12 at the Wayback Machine (Transport, Canada website page)

State of the Environment, Issue: Air Quality (Australian Government website page)

"Pollution". 11 April 2007. Archived from the original on 11 April 2007. Retrieved 1 December 2017.

Laboratory, Oak Ridge National. "Top 20 Emitting Countries by Total Fossil-Fuel CO2 Emissions for 2009". Cdiac.ornl.gov. Retrieved 1 December 2017.

Jump up to:a b Beychok, Milton R. (1967). Aqueous Wastes from Petroleum and Petrochemical Plants (1st ed.). John Wiley & Sons. ISBN 978-0-471-07189-1. LCCN 67019834.

Silent Spring, R Carlson, 1962

"Pollution Archived 2009-10-21 at the Wayback Machine". Microsoft Encarta Online Encyclopedia 2009.

"Solid Waste – The Ultimate Guide". Ppsthane.com. Retrieved 1 December 2017.

"Revolutionary CO2 maps zoom in on greenhouse gas sources". Purdue University. April 7, 2008.

"Waste Watcher" (PDF). Retrieved 2010-08-26.

Alarm sounds on US population boom. August 31, 2006. The Boston Globe.

"China overtakes US as world's biggest CO2 emitter". Guardian.co.uk. June 19, 2007.

"Ranking of the world's countries by 2008 per capita fossil-fuel CO2 emission rates.". CDIAC. 2008.

"Environmental Pollution | Chemistry Science Fair Project". www.seminarsonly.com. Retrieved 2022-06-07.

Beychok, Milton R. (January 1987). "A data base for dioxin and furan emissions from refuse incinerators". Atmospheric Environment. 21 (1): 29–36. Bibcode:1987AtmEn..21...29B. doi:10.1016/0004-6981(87)90267-8.

"Environmental disasters". www.lenntech.com. Retrieved 2022-06-07.

World Carbon Dioxide Emissions Archived 2008-03-26 at the Wayback Machine (Table 1, Report DOE/EIA-0573, 2004, Energy Information Administration)

Carbon dioxide emissions chart (graph on Mongabay website page based on Energy Information Administration's tabulated data)

"Global Warming Can Be Stopped, World Climate Experts Say". News.nationalgeographic.com. Retrieved 2010-08-26.

World Resources Institute: August 2008 Monthly Update: Air Pollution's Causes, Consequences and Solutions Archived 2009-05-01 at the Wayback Machine Submitted by Matt Kallman on Wed, 2008-08-20 18:22. Retrieved on April 17, 2009

waterhealthconnection.org Overview of Waterborne Disease Trends Archived 2008-09-05 at the Wayback Machine By Patricia L. Meinhardt, MD, MPH, MA, Author. Retrieved on April 16, 2009

Pennsylvania State University > Potential Health Effects of Pesticides. Archived 2013-08-11 at the Wayback Machine by Eric S. Lorenz. 2007.

"Indian Pediatrics". Retrieved May 1, 2008.

"UNICEF ROSA – Young child survival and development – Water and Sanitation". Retrieved 11 November 2011.

Isalkar, Umesh (29 July 2014). "Over 1,500 lives lost to diarrhoea in 2013, delay in treatment blamed". The Times of India. Indiatimes. Retrieved 29 July 2014.

"As China Roars, Pollution Reaches Deadly Extremes". The New York Times. August 26, 2007.

Wong, Edward (1 April 2013). "Air Pollution Linked to 1.2 Million Deaths in China". The New York Times. Retrieved 1 December 2017.

Maji, Kamal Jyoti; Arora, Mohit; Dikshit, Anil Kumar (2017-04-01). "Burden of disease attributed to ambient PM2.5 and PM10 exposure in 190 cities in China". Environmental Science and Pollution Research. 24 (12): 11559–11572. doi:10.1007/s11356-017-8575-7. ISSN 0944-1344. PMID 28321701. S2CID 37640939.

Chinese Air Pollution Deadliest in World, Report Says. National Geographic News. July 9, 2007.

David, Michael, and Caroline. "Air Pollution – Effects". Library.thinkquest.org. Retrieved 2010-08-26.

Stanglin, Doug (October 20, 2017). "Global pollution is the world's biggest killer and a threat to survival of mankind, study finds". USA Today. Retrieved October 20, 2017.

Mailloux, Nicholas A.; Abel, David W.; Holloway, Tracey; Patz, Jonathan A. (16 May 2022). "Nationwide and Regional PM2.5-Related Air Quality Health Benefits From the Removal of Energy-Related Emissions in the United States". GeoHealth. 6 (5): e2022GH000603. doi:10.1029/2022GH000603. PMC 9109601. PMID 35599962.

Persson, Linn; et al. (2022). "Outside the Safe Operating Space of the Planetary Boundary for Novel Entities". Environmental Science &

Technology. 56 (3): 1510–1521. Bibcode:2022EnST...56.1510P. doi:10.1021/acs.est.1c04158. PMC 8811958. PMID 35038861.

Carrington, Damian (January 18, 2022). "Chemical pollution has passed safe limit for humanity, say scientists". The Guardian. Retrieved January 18, 2022.

"SIS.nlm.nih.gov". SIS.nlm.nih.gov. 2010-08-12. Archived from the original on 2018-09-01. Retrieved 2010-08-26.

"Toxnet.nlm.nih.gov". Toxnet.nlm.nih.gov. Retrieved 2010-08-26.

Herrnstadt, Evan; Heyes, Anthony; Muehlegger, Erich; Saberian, Soodeh (2021). "Air Pollution and Criminal Activity: Microgeographic Evidence from Chicago". American Economic Journal: Applied Economics. 13 (4): 70–100. doi:10.1257/app.20190091. hdl:10871/122348. ISSN 1945-7782. S2CID 226513602.

Heissel, Jennifer; Persico, Claudia; Simon, David (2019). "Does Pollution Drive Achievement? The Effect of Traffic Pollution on Academic Performance". doi:10.3386/w25489. hdl:10945/61763. S2CID 135425218.

Zivin, Joshua Graff; Neidell, Matthew (2012-12-01). "The Impact of Pollution on Worker Productivity". American Economic Review. 102 (7): 3652–3673. doi:10.1257/aer.102.7.3652. ISSN 0002-8282. PMC 4576916. PMID 26401055.

Li, Teng; Liu, Haoming; Salvo, Alberto (2015-05-29). "Severe Air Pollution and Labor Productivity". Rochester, NY: Social Science Research Network. SSRN 2581311.

Neidell, Matthew; Gross, Tal; Graff Zivin, Joshua; Chang, Tom Y. (2019). "The Effect of Pollution on Worker Productivity: Evidence from Call Center Workers in China" (PDF). American Economic Journal: Applied Economics. 11 (1): 151–172. doi:10.1257/app.20160436. ISSN 1945-7782. S2CID 3329058.

Salvo, Alberto; Liu, Haoming; He, Jiaxiu (2019). "Severe Air Pollution and Labor Productivity: Evidence from Industrial Towns in China". American Economic Journal: Applied Economics. 11 (1): 173–201. doi:10.1257/app.20170286. ISSN 1945-7782. S2CID 41838178.

American Petroleum Institute (API) (February 1990). Management of Water Discharges: Design and Operations of Oil–Water Separators (1st ed.). American Petroleum Institute.

The staggering economic cost of air pollution By Chelsea Harvey, Washington Post, January 29, 2016

Freshwater Pollution Costs US At Least $4.3 Billion A Year, Science Daily, November 17, 2008

The human cost of China's untold soil pollution problem, The Guardian, Monday 30 June 2014 11.53 EDT

Jump up to:a b c Jonathan., Gruber (2013). Public finance and public policy (4th ed.). New York: Worth Publishers. ISBN 978-1-4292-7845-4. OCLC 819816787.

D., Kolstad, Charles (2011). Environmental economics (2nd ed.). New York: Oxford University Press. ISBN 978-0-19-973264-7. OCLC 495996799.

"Abatement and Marginal Abatement Cost (MAC)". www.econport.org. Retrieved 2018-03-07.

EPA,OA,OP,NCEE, US (31 March 2016). "Pollution Abatement Costs and Expenditures: 2005 Survey | US EPA". US EPA. Retrieved 2018-03-07.

"World's Worst Pollution Problems" (PDF).

Gabbatiss, Josh (July 18, 2018). "Meat and dairy companies to surpass oil industry as world's biggest polluters, report finds". The Independent. Retrieved June 29, 2019.

"18.1 Maximizing the Net Benefits of Pollution | Principles of Economics". open.lib.umn.edu. 17 June 2016. Retrieved 2018-03-07.

William), Pearce, David W. (David (1990). Economics of natural resources and the environment. Turner, R. Kerry. Baltimore: Johns Hopkins University Press. ISBN 978-0-8018-3987-0. OCLC 20170416.

Jump up to:a b R., Krugman, Paul (2013). Microeconomics. Wells, Robin. (3rd ed.). New York: Worth Publishers. ISBN 978-1-4292-8342-7. OCLC 796082268.

Spengler, John D.; Sexton, K. A. (1983). "Indoor Air Pollution: A Public Health Perspective". Science. 221 (4605): 9–17 [p. 9]. Bibcode:1983Sci...221....9S. doi:10.1126/science.6857273. PMID 6857273.

Hong, Sungmin; et al. (1996). "History of Ancient Copper Smelting Pollution During Roman and Medieval Times Recorded in Greenland Ice". Science. 272 (5259): 246–249 [p. 248]. Bibcode:1996Sci...272..246H. doi:10.1126/science.272.5259.246. S2CID 176767223.

David Urbinato (Summer 1994). "London's Historic "Pea-Soupers"". United States Environmental Protection Agency. Retrieved 2006-08-02.

"Deadly Smog". PBS. 2003-01-17. Retrieved 2006-08-02.

Lee Jackson, Dirty Old London: The Victorian Fight Against Filth (2014)

Cited in David Clay Large, Berlin (2000) pp 17-18

Phillips, Walter Alison (1911). "Berlin" . In Chisholm, Hugh (ed.). Encyclopædia Britannica. Vol. 03 (11th ed.). Cambridge University Press. pp. 785–791, see page 786. Dr A. Shadwell (Industrial Efficiency, London, 1906)

describes it as representing “the most complete application of science... ”

Patrick Allitt, A Climate of Crisis: America in the Age of Environmentalism (2014) p 206

Jeffry M. Diefendorf; Kurkpatrick Dorsey (2009). City, Country, Empire: Landscapes in Environmental History. University of Pittsburgh Press. pp. 44–49. ISBN 978-0-8229-7277-8.

Fleming, James R.; Knorr, Bethany R. "History of the Clean Air Act". American Meteorological Society. Retrieved 2006-02-14.

Patrick Allitt, A Climate of Crisis: America in the Age of Environmentalism (2014) pp. 15–21

1952: London fog clears after days of chaos (BBC News)

John Tarantino. "Environmental Issues". The Environmental Blog. Archived from the original on 2012-01-11. Retrieved 2011-12-10.

Judith A. Layzer, "Love Canal: hazardous waste and politics of fear" in Layzer, The Environmental Case (CQ Press, 2012) pp. 56–82.

Lenssen, "Nuclear Waste: The Problem that Won’t Go Away", Worldwatch Institute, Washington, D.C., 1991: 15.

Friedman, Sharon M. (2011). "Three Mile Island, Chernobyl, and Fukushima: An analysis of traditional and new media coverage of nuclear accidents and radiation". Bulletin of the Atomic Scientists. 67 (5): 55–65. Bibcode:2011 BuAtS..67e..55F.

doi:10.1177/0096340211421587. S2CID 145396822.

Further Reading

- Clayton, David and Michael Hills (1993) Statistical Models in Epidemiology Oxford University Press. ISBN 0-19-852221-5
- Miquel Porta, editor (2014) "A dictionary of epidemiology", 6th edn, New York: Oxford University Press.
- Morabia, Alfredo, editor. (2004) A History of Epidemiologic Methods and Concepts. Basel, Birkhauser Verlag. Part I.
- Smetanin P, Kobak P, Moyer C, Maley O (2005). "The Risk Management of Tobacco Control Research Policy Programs" The World Conference on Tobacco OR Health Conference, 12–15 July 2006, Washington DC.
- Szklo M, Nieto FJ (2002). "Epidemiology: beyond the basics", Aspen Publishers.
- Robertson LS (2015). Injury Epidemiology: Fourth Edition. Free online at nanlee.net
- Rothman K., Sander Greenland, Lash T., editors (2008). "Modern Epidemiology", 3rd Edition, Lippincott Williams & Wilkins. ISBN 0-7817-5564-6, 978-0-7817-5564-1
- Olsen J, Christensen K, Murray J, Ekbom A. An Introduction to Epidemiology for Health Professionals. New York: Springer Science+Business Media; 2010 ISBN 978-1-4419-1497-2
-
-

1. Jørn Olsen, Kaare Christensen, Jeff Murray, Anders Ekbom, 2010, An Introduction to Epidemiology for Health Professionals, Springer Series on Epidemiology and Health, Ed.: *Wolfgang Ahrens, Iris Pigeo*, pp 153
2. James F. McKenzie, Robert R. Pinger, Jerome E. Kotecki, 2005, An introduction to community health, 5th ed, Jones and Bartlett Publishers, pp 633
3. Susan Carr, Nigel Unwin and Tanja Pless-Mulloli, 2007, An Introduction to Public Health and Epidemiology, Open University Press McGraw-Hill Education, pp 190

Broad Street Outbreak

On 31 August 1854, after several other outbreaks had occurred elsewhere in the city, a major outbreak of cholera occurred in Soho. Snow later called it "the most terrible outbreak of cholera which ever occurred in this kingdom." Over the next three days, 127 people on or near Broad Street died. During the next week, three-quarters of the residents had fled the area. By 10 September, 500 people had died and the mortality rate was 12.8 percent in some parts of the city. By the end of the outbreak, 616 people had died. Many of the victims were taken to the Middlesex Hospital, where their treatment was superintended by ***Florence Nightingale***, who briefly joined the hospital in early September in order to help with the outbreak.

According to a letter from Elizabeth Gaskell, "She herself was up night and day from Friday afternoon to Sunday afternoon, receiving the poor creatures (chiefly fallen women of that neighbourhood - they had it the worst) who were being constantly brought in - - undressing them - putting on turpentine stupes, et cetera, doing it herself to as many as she could manage". By talking to local residents (with the help of Reverend Henry Whitehead), Snow identified the source of the outbreak as the public water pump on Broad Street (now Broadwick Street) at Cambridge Street. Although Snow's chemical and microscope examination of a sample of the water from this Broad Street pump water did not conclusively prove its danger, his facts about the patterns of illness and death among residents in Soho persuaded the St James parish authorities to disable the well pump by removing its handle. Although this action has been popularly reported as ending the outbreak, the epidemic may have already been in rapid decline, as explained by Snow: There is no doubt that the mortality was much diminished, as I said before, by the flight of the population, which commenced soon after the outbreak; but the attacks had so far diminished before the use of the water was stopped, that it is impossible to decide whether the well still contained the cholera poison in an active state, or whether, from some cause, the water had become free from it.

Snow later used a dot map to illustrate how cases of cholera occurred around this pump. Snow's efforts to connect the incidence of cholera with potential geographic sources were based on creating what is now known as a Voronoi diagram. He mapped the locations of individual water pumps and generated cells that represented all the points on his map which were closest to each pump. The section of Snow's map representing areas in the city where the closest available source of water was the Broad Street pump included the highest incidence of cholera cases. Snow also performed a statistical comparison between the Southwark and Vauxhall Waterworks Company, and a waterworks at Seething Wells (owned by the Lambeth Waterworks Company) that was further upriver and hence had cleaner water; he showed that houses supplied by the former had a cholera mortality rate 14 times that of those supplied by the latter. Regarding the decline in cases related to the Broad Street pump, Snow said: It will be observed that the deaths either very much diminished or ceased altogether, at every point where it becomes decidedly nearer to send to another pump than to the one in Broad Street. It may also be noticed that the deaths are most numerous near the pump where the water could be more readily obtained. There was one significant anomaly—none of the workers in the nearby Broad Street brewery contracted cholera.

As they were given a daily allowance of beer, they did not consume water from the nearby well. During the brewing process, the wort (or unfermented beer) is boiled in part so that hops can be added. This step killed the cholera bacteria in the water they had used to brew with, making it safe to drink. Snow showed that the Southwark and Vauxhall Waterworks Company was taking water from sewage-polluted sections of the Thames and delivering it to homes, resulting in an increased incidence of cholera among its customers. Snow's study is part of the history of public health and health geography. It is regarded as the founding event of epidemiology.

Smallpox Eradication

December 2022 marked 45 years since the last naturally acquired case of smallpox in the world. This last case occurred in Somalia in October 1977. Although two cases of smallpox were reported in the United Kingdom in 1978, these were associated with a research laboratory and did not represent a natural recurrence. Smallpox is caused by the variola virus. In its severest form, it is a disfiguring and deadly disease. Manifestations of the disease include fever, headache, malaise, and prostration. A rash appears and covers the body, and there is bleeding into the skin, mucous linings, and genital tract.

The circulatory system is also severely affected. Between 15% and 40% of cases die, usually within two weeks. Survivors are terribly scarred for life and are sometimes blinded. Mass vaccinations and case-finding measures by the World Health Organization (WHO), led to the eradication of smallpox from the world.

An Essential in Public Health and Epidemiology features concepts of epidemiology in a coherent and straightforward exposition. By emphasizing a unifying set of ideas, students will develop a strong foundation for understanding the principles of epidemiologic research. in public health and clinical practice, highlighted by real-world examples throughout. New coverage includes expanded information on genetic epidemiology, epidemiology and public health policy, and ethical and professional issues in epidemiology, providing a strong basis for understanding the role and importance of epidemiology in today's data-driven society.

Mihir Bhatta (M.Sc., Ph.D., FCRSD, FSASS) is a scientific worker in the field of viral research, public health, and epidemiology, especially in human immunodeficiency virus (HIV) and viral hepatitis research. He along with his co-workers published numerous research articles in national and international journals and books. At present, Dr. Bhatta is busy in the work with several life-threatening contagious viruses.

Books written by Dr. Bhatta are:

1. An Overview of Systematic Review and Meta-analysis
2. Coronaviruses: At a glance
3. HEPATITIS: VIRAL, TOXIC, ALCOHOLIC & AUTOIMMUNE
4. The Black Fungus: An overview on Mucormycosis